OUR EARTH

This is a time scale. See page 14 for explanation.

Published by WANDERER BOOKS, A Division of Simon & Schuster, Inc.
Simon & Schuster Building
1230 Avenue of the Americas, New York, New York 10020

WANDERER and colophon are registered trademarks of Simon & Schuster, Inc.
Also available in Julian Messner Library edition.
Originally published in Italian under the title LA NOSTRA TERRA
Published simultaneously in Great Britain by Hodder & Stoughton
First American Edition 1984

Manufactured in Spain by Artes Graficas, Toledo
10 9 8 7 6 5 4 3 2 1

Library of Congress Cataloging in Publication Data

Scarry, Huck.
Our earth.

Translation of: Nostra terra.
Bibliography: p.
Includes index.
1. Civilization—History—Juvenile literature.
2. Evolution—Juvenile literature. I. Title.
CB94.S2913 1984   909   83-17033
ISBN 0-671-49846-0
0-671-50016-3 (lib bdg.)
D. L. TO: 1312 -1983

This is a distance scale. See page 14 for explanation.

HUCK SCARRY
OUR EARTH

I live in the city of Geneva, Switzerland, home of many international organizations like the United Nations and the Red Cross. Geneva is "home" for people of many lands, and from my window, under one of the old city gates, I see the whole world go by!

W WANDERER BOOKS
Published by Simon & Schuster, Inc., New York

Preface

In a way, each one of us is like a star. Each of us is aglow with his own life. We all have a family, and perhaps pets, which are close and dear to us, and who go through life beside us, like planets. Each one of us is the center of his own personal universe.

From my own window I can see on the street below many other "stars." I don't know them by name; they are all distant and unfamiliar to me. Yet each star is important – immensely important to itself, and very dear to its own set of planets; the center of its own universe.

There are over four and a half billion such "stars" living on our planet today, each one a bit different, but essentially all alike. We are all like leaves on the trees, budding and maturing, and when it is time wrinkling up and falling, leaving our place for other young leaves to bud. In living we are all alike, and in living we are like everything else within our earth and without. A living thing. A changing thing.

The soil beneath our feet is living. The air we breathe is living. Even the light from the sun, which is energy, is living, too. The earth, the sun, and all the stars in the universe are living. They were once born, and they will once die, and others will be born to replace them.

This book is a story of life: about the life of the stars and of our own earth, and also about human life as well.

For all of us, in spite of our similarities, are each a bit different from the rest. We come from different parts of the earth, and we come from different parts of the earth, and we

have different ways of life, to suit where and how we live. Ultimately, we each have different thoughts.

Too often, we tend to see the world from just our own point of view: from the center of our own personal universe. It is a limited place, compared with the real one we all live

8

The view I have of the world from my own window seems tiny indeed! My window is one among millions of others in the city. From the air the world looks much different from on the ground. From space, the world looks different still. The whole city is but a dot in the country; the country just a smudge on a continent; the continent . . .

. . . only a patch on the globe!

Geneva, Switzerland

in! I hope that by getting to know about our earth, its place in the vast heavens and our place on its tiny, brittle surface, we can put aside our own personal universe, and understand better the universe of others. It would make it a better place to live . . . in the world around us!

9

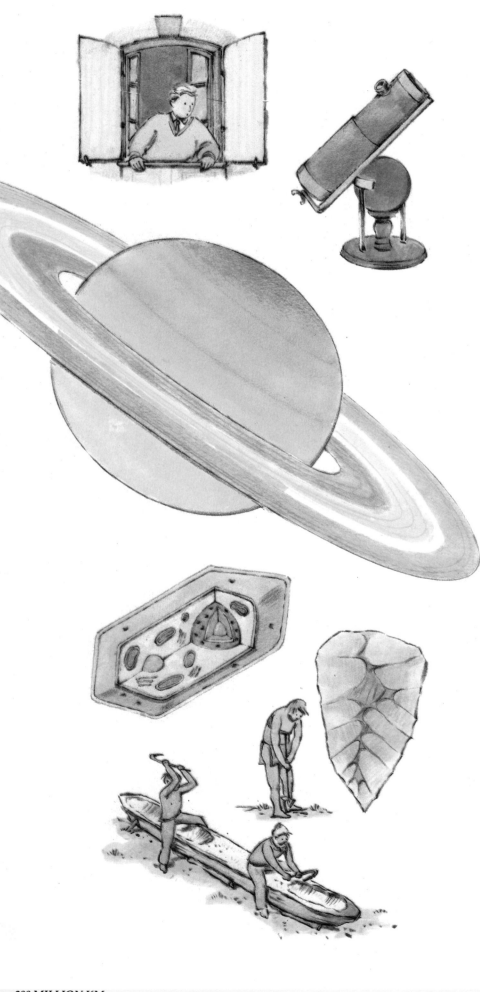

Contents

Man's View of the Earth

You have probably seen photos of the earth taken from outer space. From them you can see that the earth is like a sphere, and you can probably name the different continents on it. But these photos are very new, and until only a short time ago no one had ever seen what the earth really looked like.

Fixed with their feet on the ground, people could only see the world immediately around them, and for the rest they relied on information brought to them by others. Although man had never seen the earth from the air, his scientific mind discovered that the earth was round. He was even able to measure its size, and its distance from the sun and other planets.

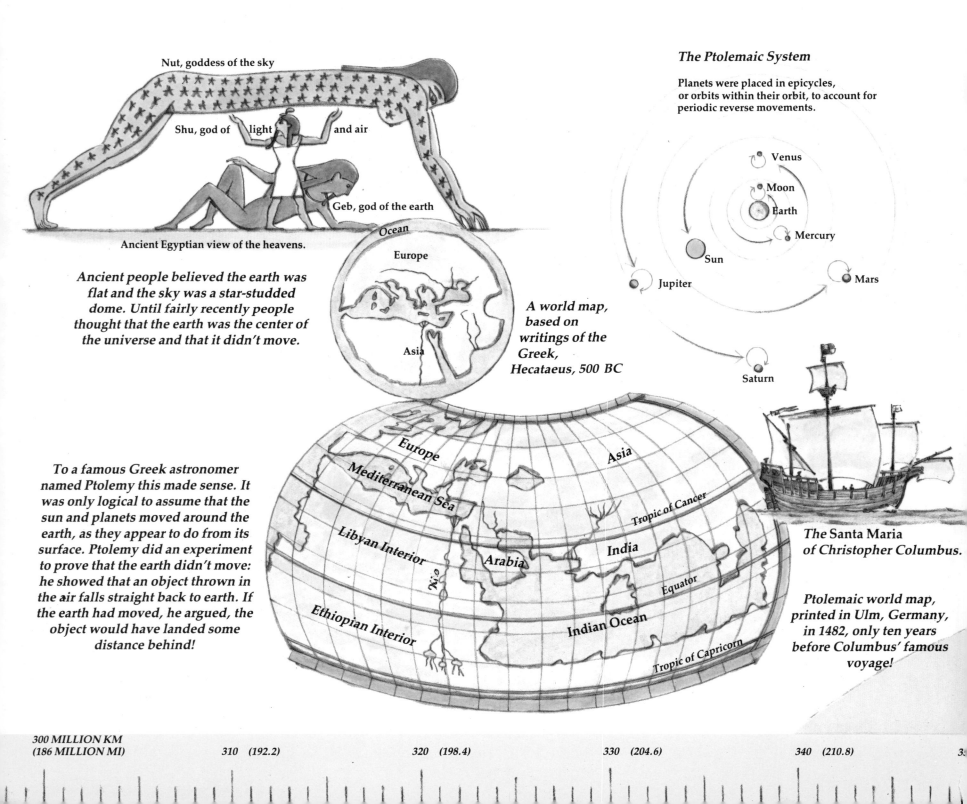

Nut, goddess of the sky

Shu, god of light and air

Geb, god of the earth

Ancient Egyptian view of the heavens.

Ancient people believed the earth was flat and the sky was a star-studded dome. Until fairly recently people thought that the earth was the center of the universe and that it didn't move.

Ocean
Europe
Asia

A world map, based on writings of the Greek, Hecataeus, 500 BC

To a famous Greek astronomer named Ptolemy this made sense. It was only logical to assume that the sun and planets moved around the earth, as they appear to do from its surface. Ptolemy did an experiment to prove that the earth didn't move: he showed that an object thrown in the air falls straight back to earth. If the earth had moved, he argued, the object would have landed some distance behind!

The Ptolemaic System

Planets were placed in epicycles, or orbits within their orbit, to account for periodic reverse movements.

Venus
Moon
Earth
Mercury
Sun
Jupiter
Mars
Saturn

Europe
Mediterranean Sea
Asia
Libyan Interior
Arabia
India
Tropic of Cancer
Nile
Ethiopian Interior
Equator
Indian Ocean
Tropic of Capricorn

The Santa Maria of Christopher Columbus.

Ptolemaic world map, printed in Ulm, Germany, in 1482, only ten years before Columbus' famous voyage!

With every new discovery, our image of the earth changes, giving a truer picture of the planet we live on. Every advancement in our knowledge of the universe rewards us with an ever smaller and seemingly insignificant place in it.

It seems an unjust reward for our curiosity!

An ancient Greek mathematician called Eratosthenes, who lived in Alexandria, Egypt, came across a bit of information in the Alexandrian Library. The paper mentioned the town of Syene, 500mi (800km) southward, where, on the longest day of the year, the summer solstice, at noon, all shadows disappear. At the bottom of a deep well one could see the sun's reflection, which was directly overhead.

Alexandria

Syene

This news interested Eratosthenes, who, at the next summer solstice, made a little experiment.

The Copernican System

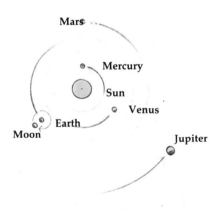

Mars

Mercury

Sun

Venus

Earth

Moon

Jupiter

Saturn

Alexandria

Syene

He erected an upright pole, but noticed, at noon, that there nonetheless was still a shadow. He concluded, since the sun's rays fall parallel to each other, that the earth must be curved . . . even round. Measuring the angle of the shadow, which was one-fiftieth of a circle, he multiplied 50 by the 500mi (800km) separating Alexandria from Syene. He arrived at 24,800mi (40,000km), very nearly the actual circumference of the earth!

A sketch of Saturn, as seen by Galileo.

The Church believed that a divinely created world should naturally sit at the center of the universe. However, as men studied the sky more carefully during the Renaissance, the Ptolemaic system showed some shortcomings. Nicholas Copernicus, for one, was disturbed by the fact that the planets appeared to stop and move backwards before resuming their paths across the night sky. Could it not be, he asked, that the earth, too, was moving, modifying our point of view? Copernicus was led to believe, after long hesitation, that this might indeed be true, and he designed a planetary chart of his own. We call it the solar system!

Galileo's original telescopes can still be seen in Florence.

Columbus was not the first man to believe that the earth was round. Ancient Greek thinkers had already observed how sailing ships gradually disappeared over the horizon, concluding, in fact, that the earth must be round. The idea was confirmed by Eratosthenes' experiment.

The lifespan of some of the people mentioned on these pages can be seen on pages 96–7.

Time Is Distance, Distance Is Time

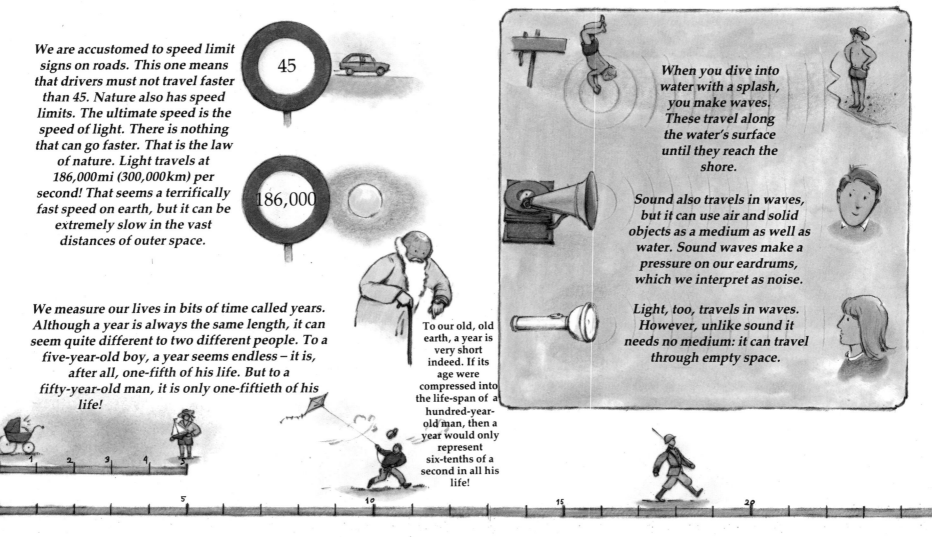

We are accustomed to speed limit signs on roads. This one means that drivers must not travel faster than 45. Nature also has speed limits. The ultimate speed is the speed of light. There is nothing that can go faster. That is the law of nature. Light travels at 186,000mi (300,000km) per second! That seems a terrifically fast speed on earth, but it can be extremely slow in the vast distances of outer space.

We measure our lives in bits of time called years. Although a year is always the same length, it can seem quite different to two different people. To a five-year-old boy, a year seems endless – it is, after all, one-fifth of his life. But to a fifty-year-old man, it is only one-fiftieth of his life!

To our old, old earth, a year is very short indeed. If its age were compressed into the life-span of a hundred-year-old man, then a year would only represent six-tenths of a second in all his life!

When you dive into water with a splash, you make waves. These travel along the water's surface until they reach the shore.

Sound also travels in waves, but it can use air and solid objects as a medium as well as water. Sound waves make a pressure on our eardrums, which we interpret as noise.

Light, too, travels in waves. However, unlike sound it needs no medium: it can travel through empty space.

Before going further into this book, I think it is important to stop for a moment to study the subject of time and distance.

If I asked you "How far is your school from home?" you might not know the answer. You would probably know how long it takes to get there though, and you might answer "Ten minutes away." Although minutes do not measure distance we can picture how far we will have travelled in ten minutes' time. So we *can* measure distance by time.

Speed is measured by combining distance and time. We know, for instance, that we are driving at sixty miles (100km) per hour, if we can travel sixty miles (100km) in the space of one hour. So time is very closely related to distance. We could even say that time *is* distance, and that distance is time!

At the top of this page, and running right through the book, I have drawn a time scale. It is like a giant ruler, measuring not inches, but years. Each notch on the scale represents not one year, nor one hundred, nor a thousand . . . but *one million years*! With this scale you can see just how long it took for living things to appear, and when human life began.

Similarly, at the bottom of the page and all

14

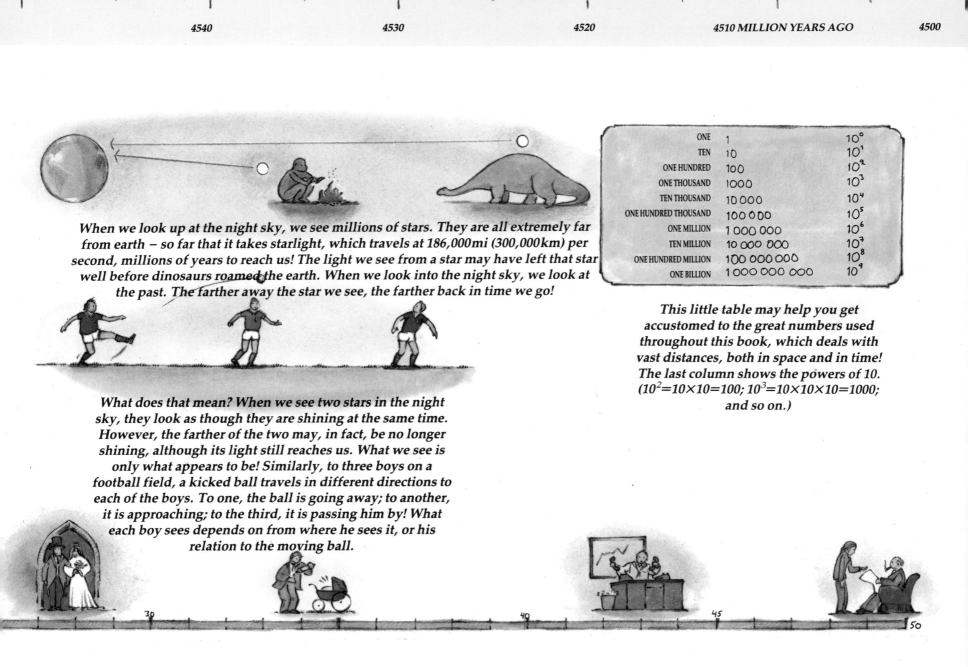

When we look up at the night sky, we see millions of stars. They are all extremely far from earth – so far that it takes starlight, which travels at 186,000mi (300,000km) per second, millions of years to reach us! The light we see from a star may have left that star well before dinosaurs roamed the earth. When we look into the night sky, we look at the past. The farther away the star we see, the farther back in time we go!

What does that mean? When we see two stars in the night sky, they look as though they are shining at the same time. However, the farther of the two may, in fact, be no longer shining, although its light still reaches us. What we see is only what appears to be! Similarly, to three boys on a football field, a kicked ball travels in different directions to each of the boys. To one, the ball is going away; to another, it is approaching; to the third, it is passing him by! What each boy sees depends on from where he sees it, or his relation to the moving ball.

ONE	1	10^0
TEN	10	10^1
ONE HUNDRED	100	10^2
ONE THOUSAND	1000	10^3
TEN THOUSAND	10 000	10^4
ONE HUNDRED THOUSAND	100 000	10^5
ONE MILLION	1 000 000	10^6
TEN MILLION	10 000 000	10^7
ONE HUNDRED MILLION	100 000 000	10^8
ONE BILLION	1 000 000 000	10^9

This little table may help you get accustomed to the great numbers used throughout this book, which deals with vast distances, both in space and in time! The last column shows the powers of 10. (10^2=10×10=100; 10^3=10×10×10=1000; and so on.)

through the book there is a distance scale. It doesn't measure either inches or even simple miles. Each notch represents *one million miles*! I have drawn the sun to the correct scale at the start, on page 6, and as you go through the pages, along the ruler, you can find the place of each of the tiny, tiny planets in our solar system . . . out as far as Neptune. (I ran out of pages for Pluto!)

Seeing the distances to be covered between one place and another in space, it becomes immediately apparent that measuring in miles or kilometers is of little use. Instead, astronomers use a much larger unit of measure, called a light-year. It is the distance light can travel in one year. (Light travels through space at 186,000 miles [300,000km] per second.) In one year, it goes about 5,878,000,000,000mi (9,460,800,000,000 km). That's far!

Our sun is about eight light-minutes away, and the moon a little less than a light-second. The next closest star is four light-years away. Our galaxy measures about 100,000 light-years across. The visible universe measures about 8,000,000,000 light-years from earth. Can you picture just how far *that* is?

15

What Is the Universe?

Perhaps the most difficult question astronomers still have to answer is "How old, and how large is the universe?" If neither the earth, nor the sun, nor even our galaxy is the center of the universe, then where is it?

Looking out at the stars, farther and farther into space (and back into time!), one asks, "How far can one go?" Does the universe spread out in every direction forever? Or does it finally stop somewhere? But if it stops, then what comes after it?

Optical telescopes can see only a limited portion of the universe, for very distant stars become too faint. Modern radio telescopes can "see" somewhat farther, but they can only pick up radio waves out to about 8 billion light-years. Beyond that is a mystery.

Today astronomers believe that distant galaxies may be moving away from our own. The farther they are, the faster they recede. At some point their speed may reach the speed of light! If this is true, then we will never know. We will never see them if their light rays never have a chance to reach us!

The theory of an expanding universe is not just a fancy, but based on careful study of the stars. The nature of different stars was studied on a spectroscope, which breaks up their light into a wide band of colors of the rainbow, called a spectrum. Those moving towards the earth showed a dominance of blue in their spectrum, while those moving away showed more red. It was found that all the distant galaxies had a dominant red spectrum, and this phenomenon, sometimes called "the red shift," led scientists to believe that these distant stars are receding, and that the universe is indeed expanding.

This theory, if correct, poses a host of new and equally difficult questions. Where is the universe expanding from? When did it start to expand? Some scientists propose that the whole universe at zero time was a tiny, dense ball of matter, which exploded in a big bang and has been growing ever since. But if there was a zero time, then what came before?

Our earth rotates around the sun, one star among 400 billion others in the Milky Way galaxy, 100,000 light-years from end to end.

It used to be thought that you could count back to the creation of the earth, following the generations listed in the Old Testament of the Bible. Our earth was thought to be about 4000 years old!

Sun ↓

The apparent size of the universe has been gradually widening as astronomers looked farther and farther into it with more powerful telescopes. There is still no end in sight!

Isaac Newton's seventeenth century reflecting telescope

A radio telescope and what it "sees"

It reads like a contour map, the tightest rings indicating a radio source: a star or galaxy.

16

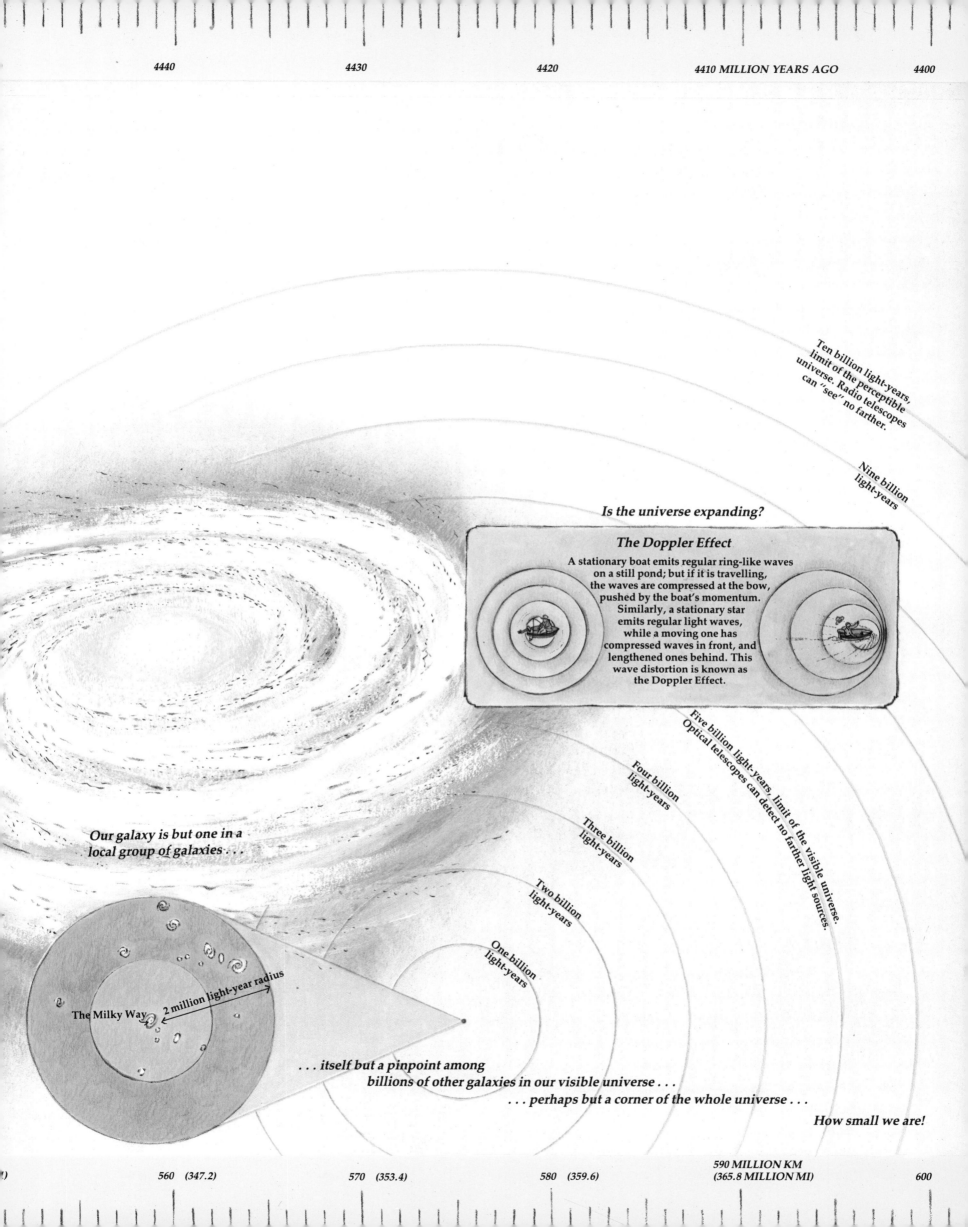

Ten billion light-years, limit of the perceptible universe. Radio telescopes can "see" no farther.

Nine billion light-years

Is the universe expanding?

The Doppler Effect

A stationary boat emits regular ring-like waves on a still pond; but if it is travelling, the waves are compressed at the bow, pushed by the boat's momentum. Similarly, a stationary star emits regular light waves, while a moving one has compressed waves in front, and lengthened ones behind. This wave distortion is known as the Doppler Effect.

Five billion light-years, limit of the visible universe. Optical telescopes can detect no farther light sources.

Four billion light-years

Three billion light-years

Our galaxy is but one in a local group of galaxies . . .

Two billion light-years

One billion light-years

The Milky Way   2 million light-year radius

. . . itself but a pinpoint among billions of other galaxies in our visible universe . . .

. . . perhaps but a corner of the whole universe . . .

How small we are!

Of Atoms and Elements

Around 400 BC , a Greek philosopher called Democritus thought that if you cut something in two, and then in two again, again and again, you would eventually come to a particle so small that it could not be cut any further. Democritus called this particle an atom (*atomos*), meaning "indivisible."

Today we know that virtually everything, from the largest stars to the tiniest microbes, is made up of billions of atoms. Atoms are the smallest components of nature. Ten million of them side by side would measure only 0.04 inch (1mm)! Yet, like outer space, they are mostly emptiness!

There are 103 different atoms. The number of protons in an atom makes it different from the others. Each different atom is a piece of a different element, or basic substance, from

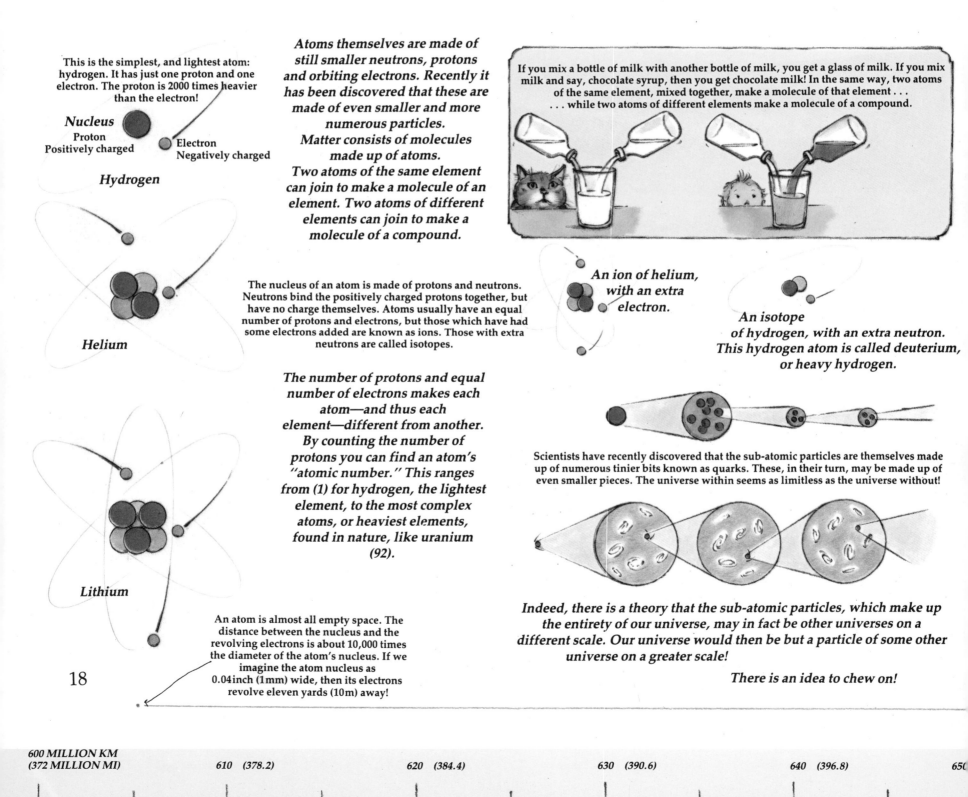

This is the simplest, and lightest atom: hydrogen. It has just one proton and one electron. The proton is 2000 times heavier than the electron!

Nucleus
Proton
Positively charged

Electron
Negatively charged

Hydrogen

Helium

Lithium

*Atoms themselves are made of still smaller neutrons, protons and orbiting electrons. Recently it has been discovered that these are made of even smaller and more numerous particles.
Matter consists of molecules made up of atoms.
Two atoms of the same element can join to make a molecule of an element. Two atoms of different elements can join to make a molecule of a compound.*

The nucleus of an atom is made of protons and neutrons. Neutrons bind the positively charged protons together, but have no charge themselves. Atoms usually have an equal number of protons and electrons, but those which have had some electrons added are known as ions. Those with extra neutrons are called isotopes.

The number of protons and equal number of electrons makes each atom—and thus each element—different from another. By counting the number of protons you can find an atom's "atomic number." This ranges from (1) for hydrogen, the lightest element, to the most complex atoms, or heaviest elements, found in nature, like uranium (92).

An atom is almost all empty space. The distance between the nucleus and the revolving electrons is about 10,000 times the diameter of the atom's nucleus. If we imagine the atom nucleus as 0.04 inch (1mm) wide, then its electrons revolve eleven yards (10m) away!

If you mix a bottle of milk with another bottle of milk, you get a glass of milk. If you mix milk and say, chocolate syrup, then you get chocolate milk! In the same way, two atoms of the same element, mixed together, make a molecule of that element . . .
. . . while two atoms of different elements make a molecule of a compound.

An ion of helium, with an extra electron.

An isotope of hydrogen, with an extra neutron. This hydrogen atom is called deuterium, or heavy hydrogen.

Scientists have recently discovered that the sub-atomic particles are themselves made up of numerous tinier bits known as quarks. These, in their turn, may be made up of even smaller pieces. The universe within seems as limitless as the universe without!

Indeed, there is a theory that the sub-atomic particles, which make up the entirety of our universe, may in fact be other universes on a different scale. Our universe would then be but a particle of some other universe on a greater scale!

There is an idea to chew on!

18

which everything is made. Most elements are natural, but man has recently modified some atoms by changing the number of protons in them, thus creating new elements.

The same elements found on earth, and within ourselves, can be found in distant stars throughout the universe. Where do atoms come from? Ultimately, all atoms come from the stars. The formation of the earth is related to that of the sun. The sun is a star, composed of gases left by earlier, exploded stars.

You and I are made up of atoms, the same ones found in the stars. In this way we are actually children of the stars, and the atoms are our link to the universe.

Isn't that wonderful?

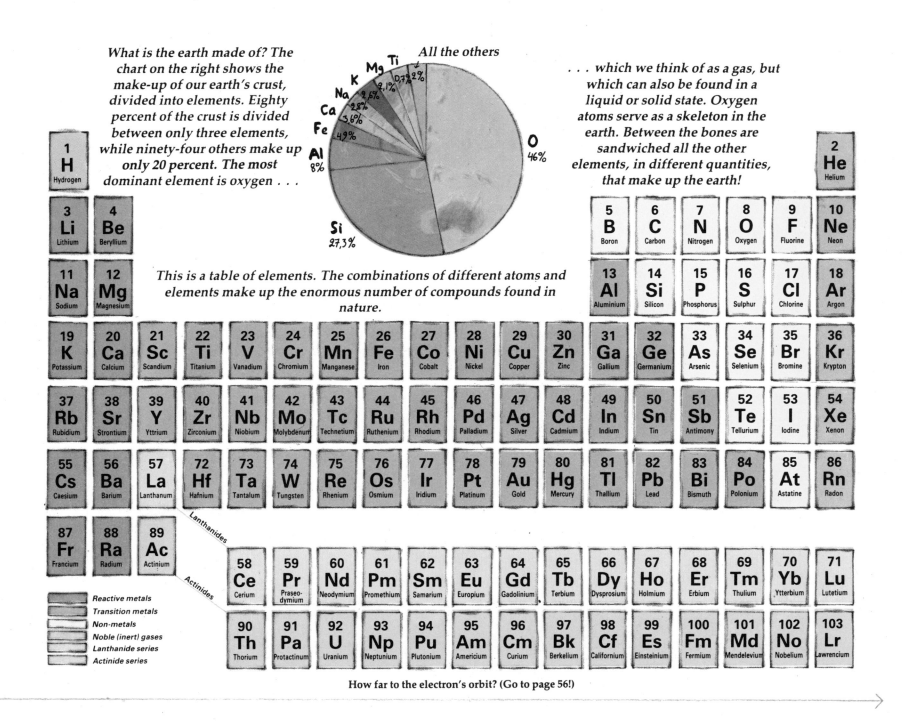

What is the earth made of? The chart on the right shows the make-up of our earth's crust, divided into elements. Eighty percent of the crust is divided between only three elements, while ninety-four others make up only 20 percent. The most dominant element is oxygen . . .

All the others

. . . which we think of as a gas, but which can also be found in a liquid or solid state. Oxygen atoms serve as a skeleton in the earth. Between the bones are sandwiched all the other elements, in different quantities, that make up the earth!

O 46%
Si 27.3%
Al 8%
Fe 4.9%
Ca 3.6%
Na 2.8%
K 2.6%
Mg 2.1%
Ti 0.7%
2%

This is a table of elements. The combinations of different atoms and elements make up the enormous number of compounds found in nature.

1 H Hydrogen	**2 He** Helium

3 Li Lithium	**4 Be** Beryllium	**5 B** Boron	**6 C** Carbon	**7 N** Nitrogen	**8 O** Oxygen

9 F Fluorine   **10 Ne** Neon

11 Na Sodium   **12 Mg** Magnesium   **13 Al** Aluminium   **14 Si** Silicon   **15 P** Phosphorus   **16 S** Sulphur   **17 Cl** Chlorine   **18 Ar** Argon

19 K Potassium   **20 Ca** Calcium   **21 Sc** Scandium   **22 Ti** Titanium   **23 V** Vanadium   **24 Cr** Chromium   **25 Mn** Manganese   **26 Fe** Iron   **27 Co** Cobalt   **28 Ni** Nickel   **29 Cu** Copper   **30 Zn** Zinc   **31 Ga** Gallium   **32 Ge** Germanium   **33 As** Arsenic   **34 Se** Selenium   **35 Br** Bromine   **36 Kr** Krypton

37 Rb Rubidium   **38 Sr** Strontium   **39 Y** Yttrium   **40 Zr** Zirconium   **41 Nb** Niobium   **42 Mo** Molybdenum   **43 Tc** Technetium   **44 Ru** Ruthenium   **45 Rh** Rhodium   **46 Pd** Palladium   **47 Ag** Silver   **48 Cd** Cadmium   **49 In** Indium   **50 Sn** Tin   **51 Sb** Antimony   **52 Te** Tellurium   **53 I** Iodine   **54 Xe** Xenon

55 Cs Caesium   **56 Ba** Barium   **57 La** Lanthanum   **72 Hf** Hafnium   **73 Ta** Tantalum   **74 W** Tungsten   **75 Re** Rhenium   **76 Os** Osmium   **77 Ir** Iridium   **78 Pt** Platinum   **79 Au** Gold   **80 Hg** Mercury   **81 Tl** Thallium   **82 Pb** Lead   **83 Bi** Bismuth   **84 Po** Polonium   **85 At** Astatine   **86 Rn** Radon

87 Fr Francium   **88 Ra** Radium   **89 Ac** Actinium

Lanthanides

Actinides

58 Ce Cerium   **59 Pr** Praseodymium   **60 Nd** Neodymium   **61 Pm** Promethium   **62 Sm** Samarium   **63 Eu** Europium   **64 Gd** Gadolinium   **65 Tb** Terbium   **66 Dy** Dysprosium   **67 Ho** Holmium   **68 Er** Erbium   **69 Tm** Thulium   **70 Yb** Ytterbium   **71 Lu** Lutetium

90 Th Thorium   **91 Pa** Protactinum   **92 U** Uranium   **93 Np** Neptunium   **94 Pu** Plutonium   **95 Am** Americium   **96 Cm** Curium   **97 Bk** Berkelium   **98 Cf** Californium   **99 Es** Einsteinium   **100 Fm** Fermium   **101 Md** Mendelevium   **102 No** Nobelium   **103 Lr** Lawrencium

Reactive metals
Transition metals
Non-metals
Noble (inert) gases
Lanthanide series
Actinide series

How far to the electron's orbit? (Go to page 56!)

The Life of the Stars

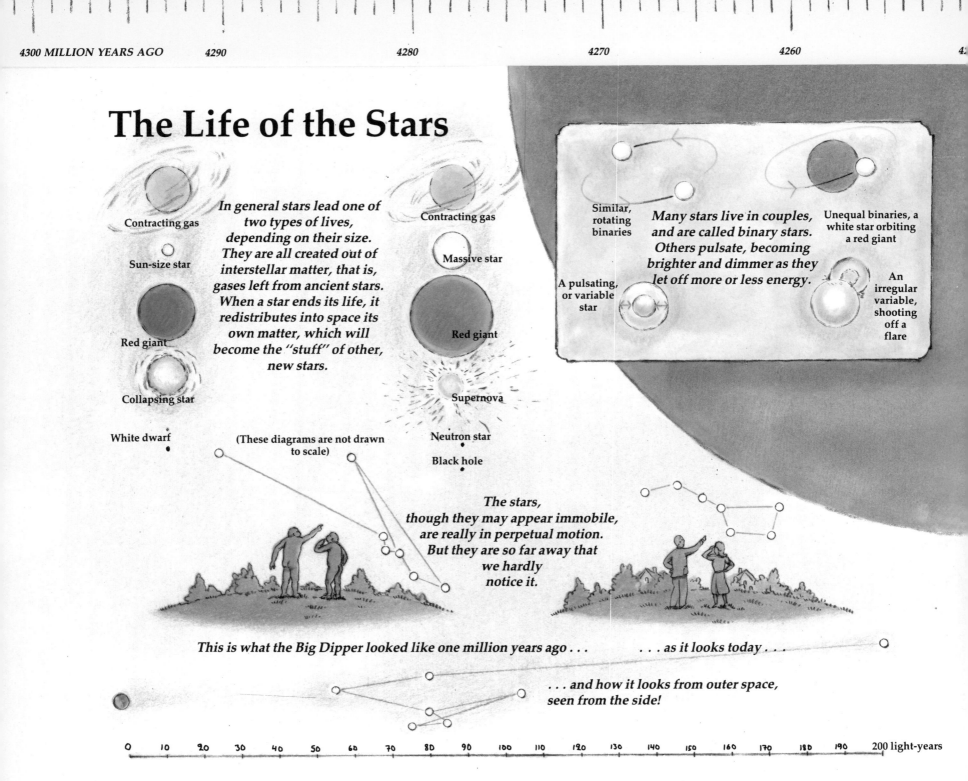

Contracting gas

Sun-size star

Red giant

Collapsing star

White dwarf

Contracting gas

Massive star

Red giant

Supernova

Neutron star

Black hole

In general stars lead one of two types of lives, depending on their size. They are all created out of interstellar matter, that is, gases left from ancient stars. When a star ends its life, it redistributes into space its own matter, which will become the "stuff" of other, new stars.

(These diagrams are not drawn to scale)

Similar, rotating binaries

A pulsating, or variable star

Many stars live in couples, and are called binary stars. Others pulsate, becoming brighter and dimmer as they let off more or less energy.

Unequal binaries, a white star orbiting a red giant

An irregular variable, shooting off a flare

The stars, though they may appear immobile, are really in perpetual motion. But they are so far away that we hardly notice it.

This is what the Big Dipper looked like one million years ago . . .   . . . as it looks today . . .

. . . and how it looks from outer space, seen from the side!

0   10   20   30   40   50   60   70   80   90   100   110   120   130   140   150   160   170   180   190   200 light-years

Stars have long been thought of as eternal. Indeed from earth they seem immovable and unchanging, and for centuries they have been reliable markers for mariners navigating the seas. Yet, just like you and me, the stars are alive and changing.

How are stars born? Floating around in the universe are great clouds of dust and gas, the remains of ancient stars. Over millions of years a cloud may condense. As it packs

together, the molecules may be pressed so tightly that they collide with one another, and generate heat.

If it gets hot enough then the hydrogen atoms in the gas fuse, in a nuclear reaction, into helium. The change in structure emits huge energy, which we see as light. A star is born!

An average star, like our sun, may burn its hydrogen for as long as ten billion years. But

20

Here, drawn to scale, are the
comparative sizes of a red giant
and our sun
(250:1).

Sun: 100 times larger than . . .

White dwarf: 700 times larger than . . .

Neutron star: 3 times larger than . . .

Black hole

The Milky Way
is a spiral galaxy.

Elliptical galaxies

Spiral galaxies

Barred galaxies

Stars are
usually born in groups
and live in great families of
about 100 billion members, called
galaxies. Galaxies are in constant
motion, spinning on their own axes,
while they move as a pack through
space. Our sun, and we with it, makes
one full turn through our galaxy
every 250 million years! There are
many different types of galaxies,
which have been classed in
groups. We do not know
if one type evolves
into another.

The gravity of a black hole is so great that
it could suck in the matter of even the
most massive stars!

at some point the fuel runs low. When this happens the star cools, shedding its outer layers, and bloating into a red giant.

Medium-sized stars like the sun then become unstable, eject their matter into space, and finish their days as a tiny, pale white dwarf.

Bigger stars experience a more violent end. After their red giant stage, they explode as a supernova, and the leftovers contract into dense neutron stars, measuring only a few miles across! They are so dense that a handful may weigh many tons. Their gravity may be so great that *nothing* can escape them, not even light. Virtually invisible, they are called black holes and in spite of their small size, they are frighteningly powerful, for their gravity can suck up anything that crosses their path . . . even other stars!

21

The Vital Sun

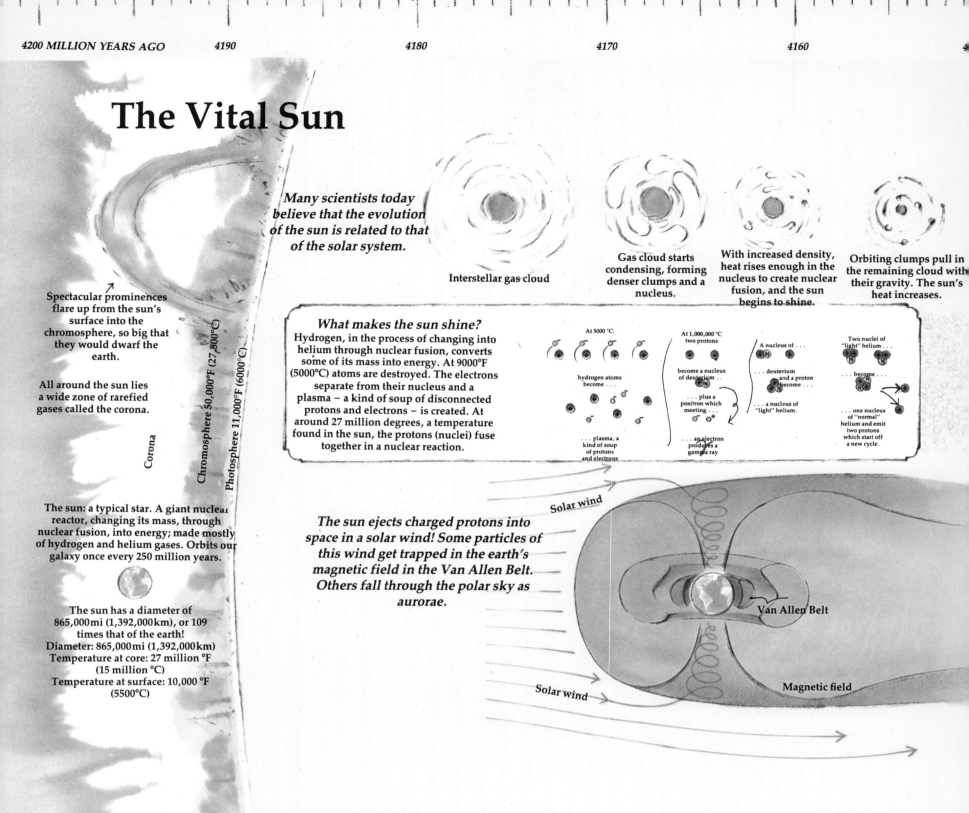

Spectacular prominences flare up from the sun's surface into the chromosphere, so big that they would dwarf the earth.

All around the sun lies a wide zone of rarefied gases called the corona.

Corona

Chromosphere 50,000°F (27,800°C)

Photosphere 11,000°F (6000°C)

The sun: a typical star. A giant nuclear reactor, changing its mass, through nuclear fusion, into energy; made mostly of hydrogen and helium gases. Orbits our galaxy once every 250 million years.

The sun has a diameter of 865,000mi (1,392,000km), or 109 times that of the earth!
Diameter: 865,000mi (1,392,000km)
Temperature at core: 27 million °F (15 million °C)
Temperature at surface: 10,000 °F (5500°C)

Many scientists today believe that the evolution of the sun is related to that of the solar system.

Interstellar gas cloud

Gas cloud starts condensing, forming denser clumps and a nucleus.

With increased density, heat rises enough in the nucleus to create nuclear fusion, and the sun begins to shine.

Orbiting clumps pull in the remaining cloud with their gravity. The sun's heat increases.

What makes the sun shine?

Hydrogen, in the process of changing into helium through nuclear fusion, converts some of its mass into energy. At 9000°F (5000°C) atoms are destroyed. The electrons separate from their nucleus and a plasma – a kind of soup of disconnected protons and electrons – is created. At around 27 million degrees, a temperature found in the sun, the protons (nuclei) fuse together in a nuclear reaction.

At 5000 °C:

hydrogen atoms become . . .

. . . plasma, a kind of soup of protons and electrons

At 1,000,000 °C two protons

become a nucleus of deuterium . . .

. . . plus a positron which meeting . . .

. . . an electron produces a gamma ray

A nucleus of . . .

. . . deuterium and a proton become . . .

. . . a nucleus of "light" helium.

Two nuclei of "light" helium . . .

. . . become . . .

. . . one nucleus of "normal" helium and emit two protons which start off a new cycle.

The sun ejects charged protons into space in a solar wind! Some particles of this wind get trapped in the earth's magnetic field in the Van Allen Belt. Others fall through the polar sky as aurorae.

Solar wind

Solar wind

Van Allen Belt

Magnetic field

Doubtless you have heard that the three vital necessities for man are food, clothing, and shelter. But have you ever thought how you could live without the sun? The sun is *the* vital necessity, not only for man, but also for every plant and every animal.

Imagine a morning that the sun didn't rise. The day would be absolutely dark. Even if there was a full moon we wouldn't see it, for it would reflect no sunlight. Without sunlight plants could not grow, and without plants, which carry out a process called photosynthesis, we would run out of air to breathe.

But alas, even before we had time to worry about our plants, death would already be at our doorstep! Even though we could keep on our electric lights, we'd notice the earth quickly growing colder and colder, deprived of the sun's warming rays. In no time everything would freeze. Lakes, rivers, even the oceans would turn as hard as ice. So would

22

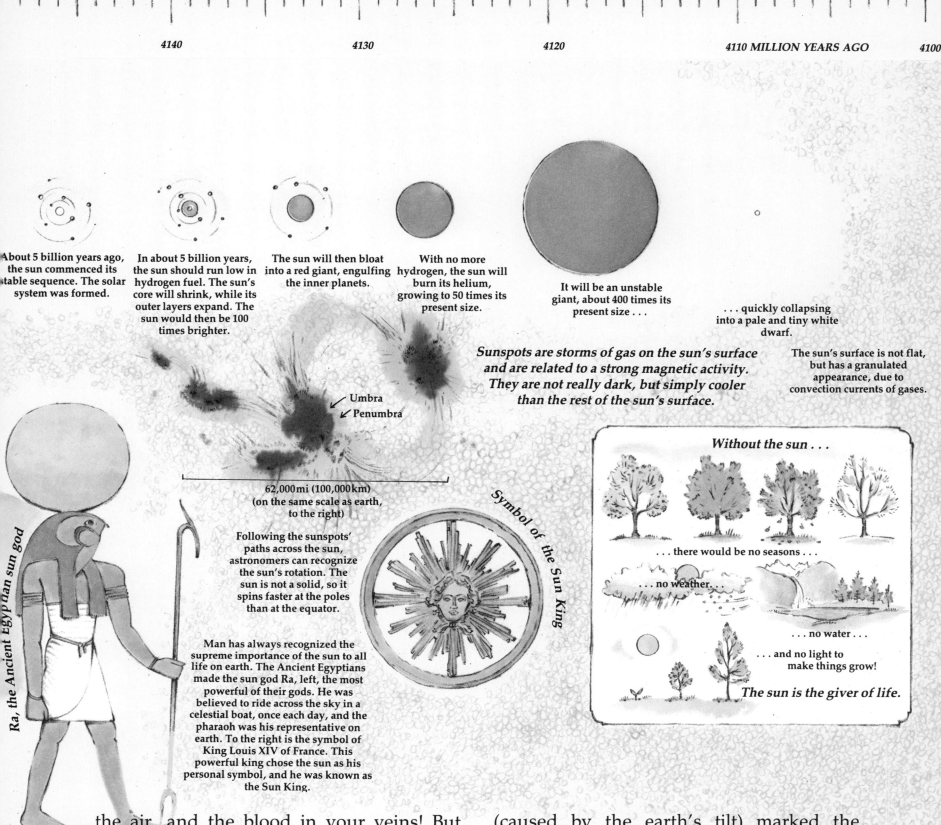

About 5 billion years ago, the sun commenced its stable sequence. The solar system was formed.

In about 5 billion years, the sun should run low in hydrogen fuel. The sun's core will shrink, while its outer layers expand. The sun would then be 100 times brighter.

The sun will then bloat into a red giant, engulfing the inner planets.

With no more hydrogen, the sun will burn its helium, growing to 50 times its present size.

It will be an unstable giant, about 400 times its present size . . .

. . . quickly collapsing into a pale and tiny white dwarf.

Sunspots are storms of gas on the sun's surface and are related to a strong magnetic activity. They are not really dark, but simply cooler than the rest of the sun's surface.

The sun's surface is not flat, but has a granulated appearance, due to convection currents of gases.

Umbra
Penumbra

62,000mi (100,000km)
(on the same scale as earth, to the right)

Following the sunspots' paths across the sun, astronomers can recognize the sun's rotation. The sun is not a solid, so it spins faster at the poles than at the equator.

Symbol of the Sun King

Ra, the Ancient Egyptian sun god

Man has always recognized the supreme importance of the sun to all life on earth. The Ancient Egyptians made the sun god Ra, left, the most powerful of their gods. He was believed to ride across the sky in a celestial boat, once each day, and the pharaoh was his representative on earth. To the right is the symbol of King Louis XIV of France. This powerful king chose the sun as his personal symbol, and he was known as the Sun King.

Without the sun . . .

. . . there would be no seasons . . .

. . . no weather . . .

. . . no water . . .

. . . and no light to make things grow!

The sun is the giver of life.

the air, and the blood in your veins! But don't worry about these chilling thoughts. The sun should keep rising each morning for at least another five billion years.

It is not surprising that ancient and primitive civilizations worshipped a sun god. They fully recognized our dependency on this great giver of life. Dates of the year which pass scarcely noticed today were an occasion for great celebration in the past. The shortest and longest days of the year

(caused by the earth's tilt) marked the cycles of life (spring and summer), and death (autumn and winter).

It is interesting to note that even our Christmas, celebrating the birth of Christ, falls within a few days of the winter solstice (December 22nd), the shortest day of the year . . . and the celebration of the rebirth of the sun, with the progressive growing and warming of each new day.

23

Earth's Neighborhood, the Solar System

In ancient times the night sky was believed to be a giant canopy of fixed stars which revolved around the earth. The Ancient Greeks enjoyed studying the stars, and on the canopy they joined groups of stars with lines to form pictures. These pictures we call constellations.

However, they noticed that some of the brightest stars moved a bit each night, crossing from one constellation to another. The Greeks called these stars *planetes*, which meant "wanderers." They could see five wanderers in the sky, without telescopes, and they were named: Mercury, Venus, Mars, Jupiter, and Saturn.

Until the sixteenth century people believed that the planets revolved around the earth. Then a Polish astronomer called Copernicus discovered that all the planets, including our own earth, revolve around the sun. A new name was needed to describe this. We call it the solar system.

We know now that there are more than five planets in the solar system. A full count of the sun's family would run like this:

Although it may look like a crowded family the solar system is mostly empty space. The sun alone accounts for about 99 percent of its total mass!

Many planets have orbiting moons. Some of Jupiter's moons are bigger than the planet Mercury, while other moons may measure only some 60mi (100km) wide. We now believe that the whole solar system was created at roughly the same time.

Only our own planet earth is suitable for us to live on. The other planets are either too cold, or too hot, have not enough air or water, or too much gravity. But some have numerous similarities with our own. It is quite possible that other planets, even if no life is found there today, may have once been home for some other form of life. It may also be possible that primitive life is burgeoning on another planet in our system right now! But no other planet, from space, shows such richness, variety and beauty as our own.

Planets	Nine
Moons (planetary satellites)	Thirty-three at least
Asteroids	Several thousand
Comets	Several dozen
Meteorites and meteors	Millions

Explanatory note: Figures for gravity are based upon earth's gravity=1. Figures for density are based on water=1.

The solar system, as far out as Neptune, is drawn to scale all along the bottom of the pages of this book. Isn't it a big and empty place?

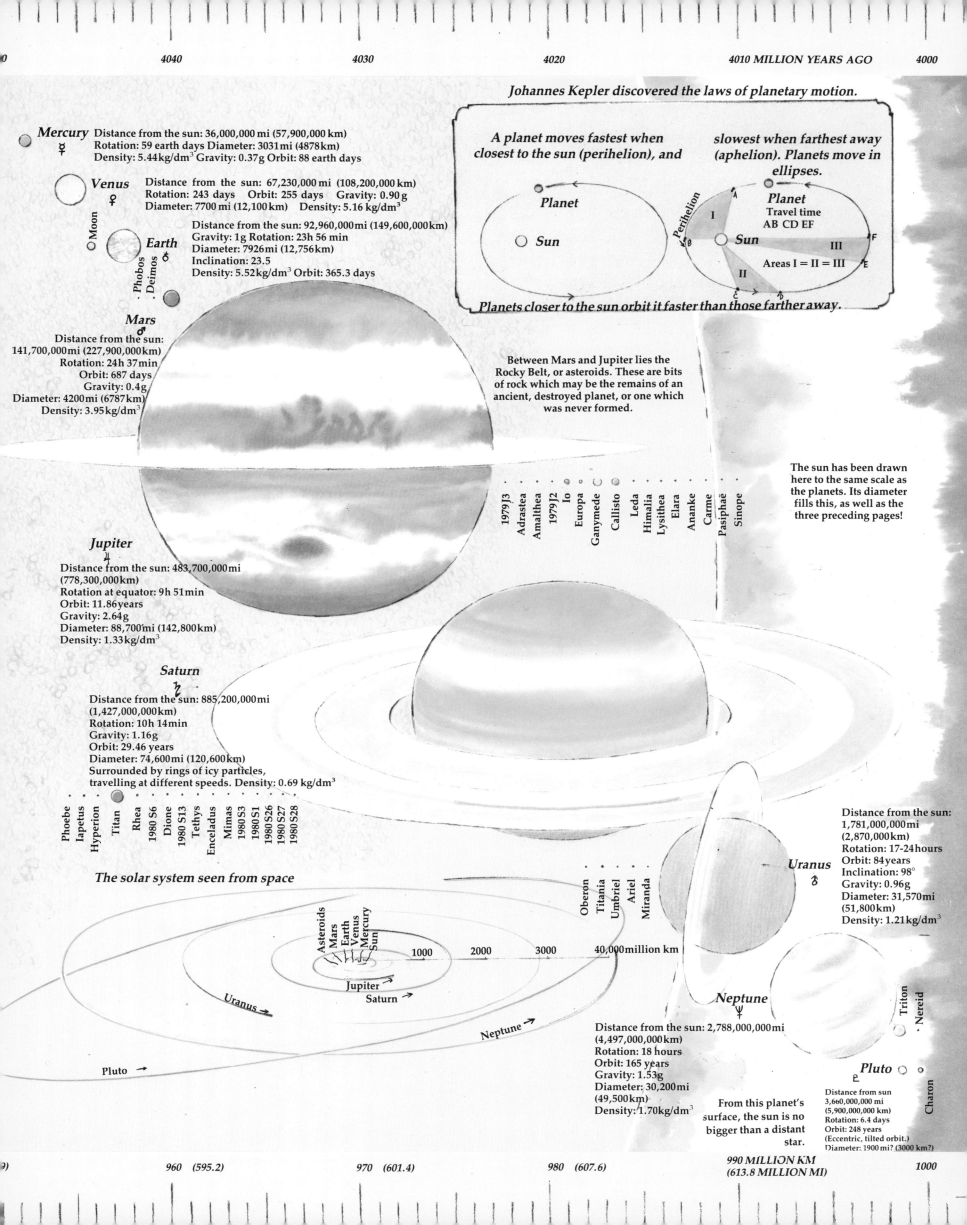

Johannes Kepler discovered the laws of planetary motion.

A planet moves fastest when closest to the sun (perihelion), and slowest when farthest away (aphelion). Planets move in ellipses.

Planet

Sun

Perihelion

Planet
Travel time
AB CD EF

Sun

Areas I = II = III

Planets closer to the sun orbit it faster than those farther away.

Mercury ☿
Distance from the sun: 36,000,000 mi (57,900,000 km)
Rotation: 59 earth days Diameter: 3031 mi (4878km)
Density: 5.44 kg/dm³ Gravity: 0.37g Orbit: 88 earth days

Venus ♀
Distance from the sun: 67,230,000 mi (108,200,000 km)
Rotation: 243 days   Orbit: 255 days   Gravity: 0.90 g
Diameter: 7700 mi (12,100 km)   Density: 5.16 kg/dm³

Moon

Earth ♁
Distance from the sun: 92,960,000 mi (149,600,000 km)
Gravity: 1g Rotation: 23h 56 min
Diameter: 7926 mi (12,756 km)
Inclination: 23.5
Density: 5.52 kg/dm³ Orbit: 365.3 days

Phobos Deimos

Mars ♂
Distance from the sun:
141,700,000 mi (227,900,000 km)
Rotation: 24h 37 min
Orbit: 687 days
Gravity: 0.4g
Diameter: 4200 mi (6787 km)
Density: 3.95 kg/dm³

Between Mars and Jupiter lies the Rocky Belt, or asteroids. These are bits of rock which may be the remains of an ancient, destroyed planet, or one which was never formed.

The sun has been drawn here to the same scale as the planets. Its diameter fills this, as well as the three preceding pages!

1979J3 · Adrastea · Amalthea · 1979J2 · Io · Europa · Ganymede · Callisto · Leda · Himalia · Lysithea · Elara · Ananke · Carme · Pasiphaë · Sinope

Jupiter ♃
Distance from the sun: 483,700,000 mi
(778,300,000 km)
Rotation at equator: 9h 51 min
Orbit: 11.86 years
Gravity: 2.64g
Diameter: 88,700 mi (142,800 km)
Density: 1.33 kg/dm³

Saturn ♄
Distance from the sun: 885,200,000 mi
(1,427,000,000 km)
Rotation: 10h 14 min
Gravity: 1.16g
Orbit: 29.46 years
Diameter: 74,600 mi (120,600 km)
Surrounded by rings of icy particles,
travelling at different speeds. Density: 0.69 kg/dm³

Phoebe · Iapetus · Hyperion · Titan · Rhea · 1980 S6 · Dione · 1980 S13 · Tethys · Enceladus · Mimas · 1980 S3 · 1980 S1 · 1980 S26 · 1980 S27 · 1980 S28

The solar system seen from space

Asteroids · Mars · Earth · Venus · Mercury · Sun

1000   2000   3000   40,000 million km

Jupiter

Saturn

Uranus

Neptune

Pluto

Oberon · Titania · Umbriel · Ariel · Miranda

Uranus ⛢
Distance from the sun:
1,781,000,000 mi
(2,870,000 km)
Rotation: 17-24 hours
Orbit: 84 years
Inclination: 98°
Gravity: 0.96g
Diameter: 31,570 mi
(51,800 km)
Density: 1.21 kg/dm³

Neptune ♆
Distance from the sun: 2,788,000,000 mi
(4,497,000,000 km)
Rotation: 18 hours
Orbit: 165 years
Gravity: 1.53g
Diameter: 30,200 mi
(49,500 km)
Density: 1.70 kg/dm³

From this planet's surface, the sun is no bigger than a distant star.

Triton · Nereid

Pluto ♇
Distance from sun
3,660,000,000 mi
(5,900,000,000 km)
Rotation: 6.4 days
Orbit: 248 years
(Eccentric, tilted orbit.)
Diameter: 1900 mi? (3000 km?)

Charon

The Moon

The silvery moon is earth's closest relative in the solar system. On first sight there is little their two faces have in common, but the moon influences so much of what happens here on earth that we might call it earth's little brother.

We know that the moon orbits the earth, held by the earth's gravity. But the moon's gravity is also tugging on earth, and in fact both bodies revolve around a barycenter, or an in-between point between their axes. The moon's gravity tugs at the water in our oceans, and as it and the earth revolve, creates the tides.

The regular waning and waxing of the moon enabled ancient peoples to measure weeks and months. (The word "month" comes from "moon.") Although the moon's radius is only a quarter that of the earth's, it is proportionately much larger than the

If we were to take a long cord and pull the moon alongside our planet, like a dinghy to a ship, here is how big our nearest neighbor in space would look!

Earth's diameter, for comparison: 7927mi (12,756km)

The Moon

Distance from the earth: 238,900mi (384,000km)
Diameter: 2160mi (3476km)
Day temperature: 214°F to 266°F (101° to 130°C)
By night – 307°F (–153°C)

The great, flat, circular maria, or seas, may have been created by the impact of a large, massive body, or meteorite, which dug so deep that lava welled up from within and filled up its own crater.

There are mountain ranges on the moon as lofty as those found on earth. Those in the Apennines rise to more than 21,300ft (6500m).

Craters are formed either by striking objects or by volcanoes.

On a clear night, take a pair of binoculars and look at the moon. It is a fascinating sight!

26

moons' of any of the other planets. Since it exerts so much influence on earth, some scientists consider the earth and moon as a binary planet system.

Scientists believe that the moon was formed in a similar manner to the other planets of the solar system, from bits of condensing matter pulled together by gravity. The moon's gravity is only about one-sixth that on earth, too little to hold down an atmosphere. There is no air and no water there.

The most striking feature of the moon is its craters. Where do they come from? Many craters are made by the impact of meteorites or other bodies crashing on its surface. Probably if the earth had no atmosphere in which falling meteors can burn up by friction it would have a rather similar pockmarked surface! Other craters are the remnants of

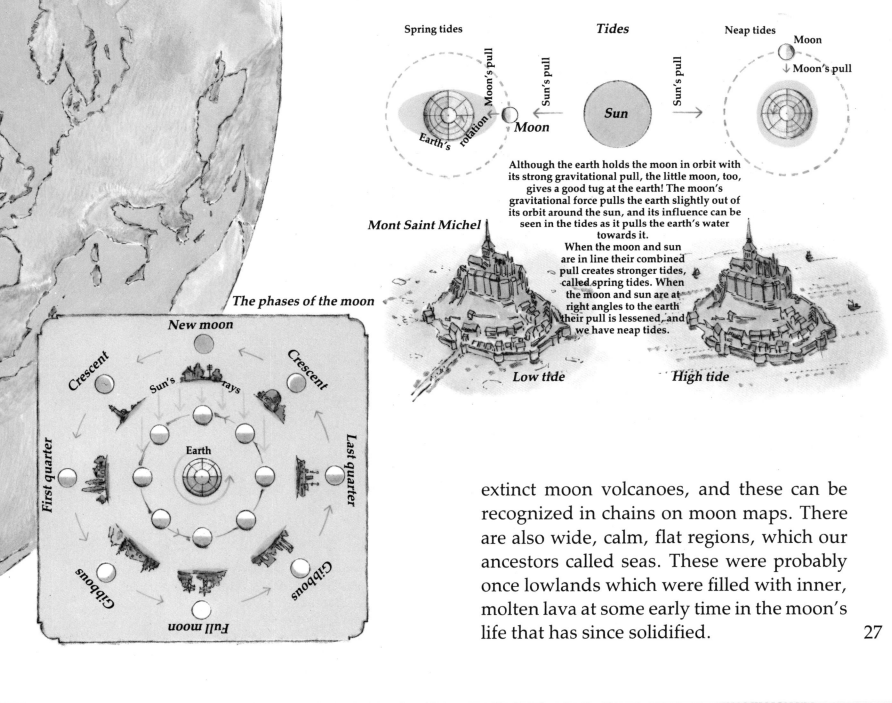

Tides

Although the earth holds the moon in orbit with its strong gravitational pull, the little moon, too, gives a good tug at the earth! The moon's gravitational force pulls the earth slightly out of its orbit around the sun, and its influence can be seen in the tides as it pulls the earth's water towards it.
When the moon and sun are in line their combined pull creates stronger tides, called spring tides. When the moon and sun are at right angles to the earth their pull is lessened, and we have neap tides.

The phases of the moon

extinct moon volcanoes, and these can be recognized in chains on moon maps. There are also wide, calm, flat regions, which our ancestors called seas. These were probably once lowlands which were filled with inner, molten lava at some early time in the moon's life that has since solidified.

27

Heavenly Clockwork: the Earth-Moon-Sun System

Every day throughout the year we ride on the hands of a giant celestial clock. This clock tells us when it is day, when it is night, when the tide is high, and what season we're in. It has only three gears . . . the sun, the moon and the earth.

How does it work? The clock runs on two natural forces: gravity and centrifugal force. The sun's gravity pulls on the earth, but the earth propels itself through space and the momentum pulls it away from the sun's gravity. The two forces are just strong enough to equalize each other: the sun keeping the earth from flying away, and the earth's momentum keeping it from falling into the sun. The earth is held, then, in orbit.

The moon orbits the earth in just the same way. One orbit of the earth around the sun makes one year, and one orbit of the moon around the earth makes one lunar month.

While the earth and moon are in their orbits they are spinning like tops on an axis. One spin around is called a rotation. The earth makes one rotation in about twenty-four hours, making one day, while the moon takes twenty-seven earth days to make just one rotation.

The earth's axis of rotation is not perpendicular to its orbit around the sun. If it were, then every day of the year would receive the same amount of sunlight. Instead the earth rides its orbit (called the ecliptic) with a tilt, so that the length of days throughout the year are never equal. This tilt gives us the seasons.

Before the recent age of mechanical clocks and watches, the only way to tell time or

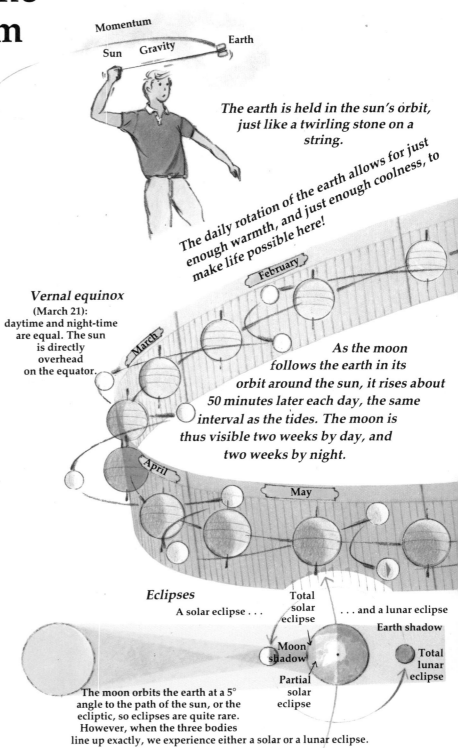

The earth is held in the sun's orbit, just like a twirling stone on a string.

The daily rotation of the earth allows for just enough warmth, and just enough coolness, to make life possible here!

Vernal equinox (March 21): daytime and night-time are equal. The sun is directly overhead on the equator.

As the moon follows the earth in its orbit around the sun, it rises about 50 minutes later each day, the same interval as the tides. The moon is thus visible two weeks by day, and two weeks by night.

Eclipses

A solar eclipse . . .   Total solar eclipse   . . . and a lunar eclipse

Earth shadow

Moon shadow   Total lunar eclipse

Partial solar eclipse

The moon orbits the earth at a 5° angle to the path of the sun, or the ecliptic, so eclipses are quite rare. However, when the three bodies line up exactly, we experience either a solar or a lunar eclipse.

know the date was to read the celestial clock. People counted the time from one full moon to the next and sometimes built in their temples a marker which the sun might light only once a year.

28

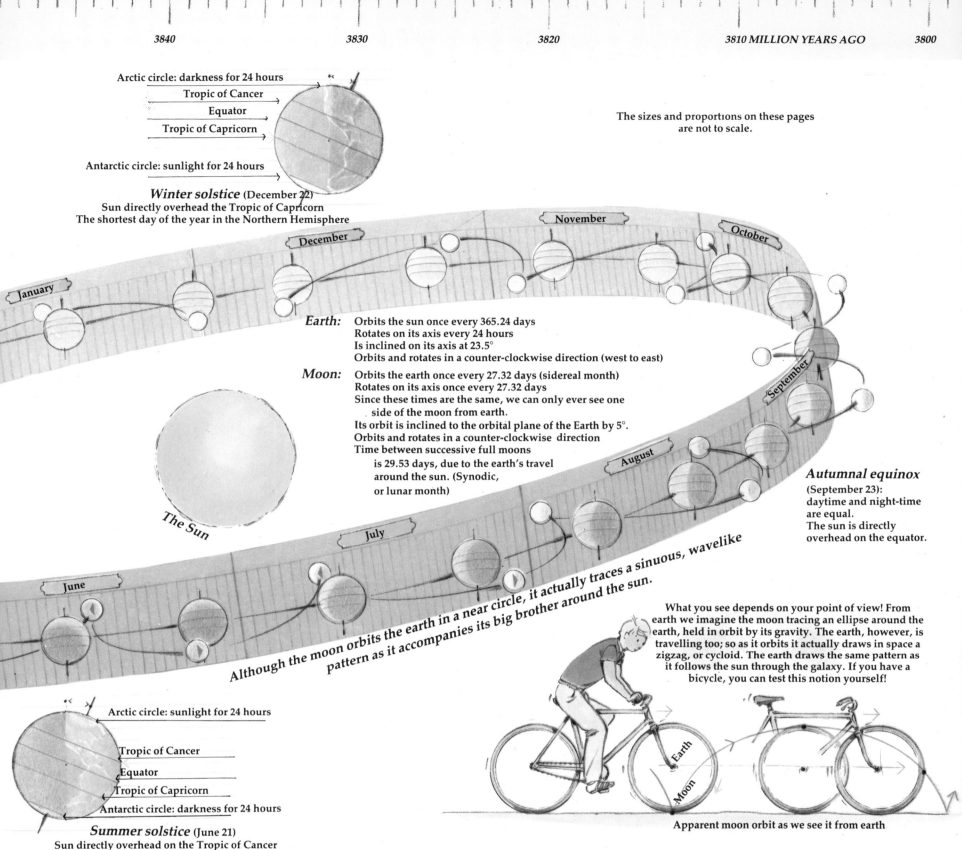

Arctic circle: darkness for 24 hours
Tropic of Cancer
Equator
Tropic of Capricorn

Antarctic circle: sunlight for 24 hours

Winter solstice (December 22)
Sun directly overhead the Tropic of Capricorn
The shortest day of the year in the Northern Hemisphere

The sizes and proportions on these pages
are not to scale.

November

October

December

January

Earth: Orbits the sun once every 365.24 days
Rotates on its axis every 24 hours
Is inclined on its axis at 23.5°
Orbits and rotates in a counter-clockwise direction (west to east)

Moon: Orbits the earth once every 27.32 days (sidereal month)
Rotates on its axis once every 27.32 days
Since these times are the same, we can only ever see one
   side of the moon from earth.
Its orbit is inclined to the orbital plane of the Earth by 5°.
Orbits and rotates in a counter-clockwise direction
Time between successive full moons
   is 29.53 days, due to the earth's travel
   around the sun. (Synodic,
   or lunar month)

September

The Sun

July

August

Autumnal equinox
(September 23):
daytime and night-time
are equal.
The sun is directly
overhead on the equator.

June

Although the moon orbits the earth in a near circle, it actually traces a sinuous, wavelike
pattern as it accompanies its big brother around the sun.

What you see depends on your point of view! From
earth we imagine the moon tracing an ellipse around the
earth, held in orbit by its gravity. The earth, however, is
travelling too; so as it orbits it actually draws in space a
zigzag, or cycloid. The earth draws the same pattern as
it follows the sun through the galaxy. If you have a
bicycle, you can test this notion yourself!

Earth

Moon

Apparent moon orbit as we see it from earth

Arctic circle: sunlight for 24 hours

Tropic of Cancer
Equator
Tropic of Capricorn
Antarctic circle: darkness for 24 hours

Summer solstice (June 21)
Sun directly overhead on the Tropic of Cancer
The longest day of the year in the Northern Hemisphere

Although the ancients needed no clocks to catch a train, they depended on exact knowledge of the march of the seasons. Knowing just when to plant and when to harvest might be an affair of life or death! By keeping careful track of the year the Ancient Egyptians, for instance, knew when the Nile River would flood, so they could open their irrigation sluice gates to feed their crops with water.

29

Meet Planet Earth!

We are very lucky to live on earth. It is certainly the most unusual and most beautiful planet in the solar system. If a space traveller ever came close enough to our sun to distinguish the planets, there is little doubt that he would be intrigued enough to take a closer look at the brilliant blue sapphire, veiled in swirling cotton clouds, which is our planet.

What makes our planet unique among others is that it is the only place we know of where life exists. There are other planets with an atmosphere, and with water locked up as ice, but none has just the right combination of oxygen, water and sunshine to make life as we know it possible.

If the earth rotated just a bit slower, the days would be intolerably hot and life might not be possible. If the earth orbited the sun a bit closer to Mars, it would be impossibly cold! If the earth had been bigger, more massive, its gravity might have held down hydrogen gas, rendering our atmosphere poisonous. Had the earth been smaller, its gravity might not have held any atmosphere at all, and our planet might have looked like the pockmarked moon!

The earth is a very small and rare place, and we can only exist on the thin film of its surface. Such a unique planet merits our respect, and care for its preservation.

The North American continent lies opposite . . .

The watery North Pole is surrounded by continents . . .

The great African continent . . .

All life exists within this thin band of air, soil and water!

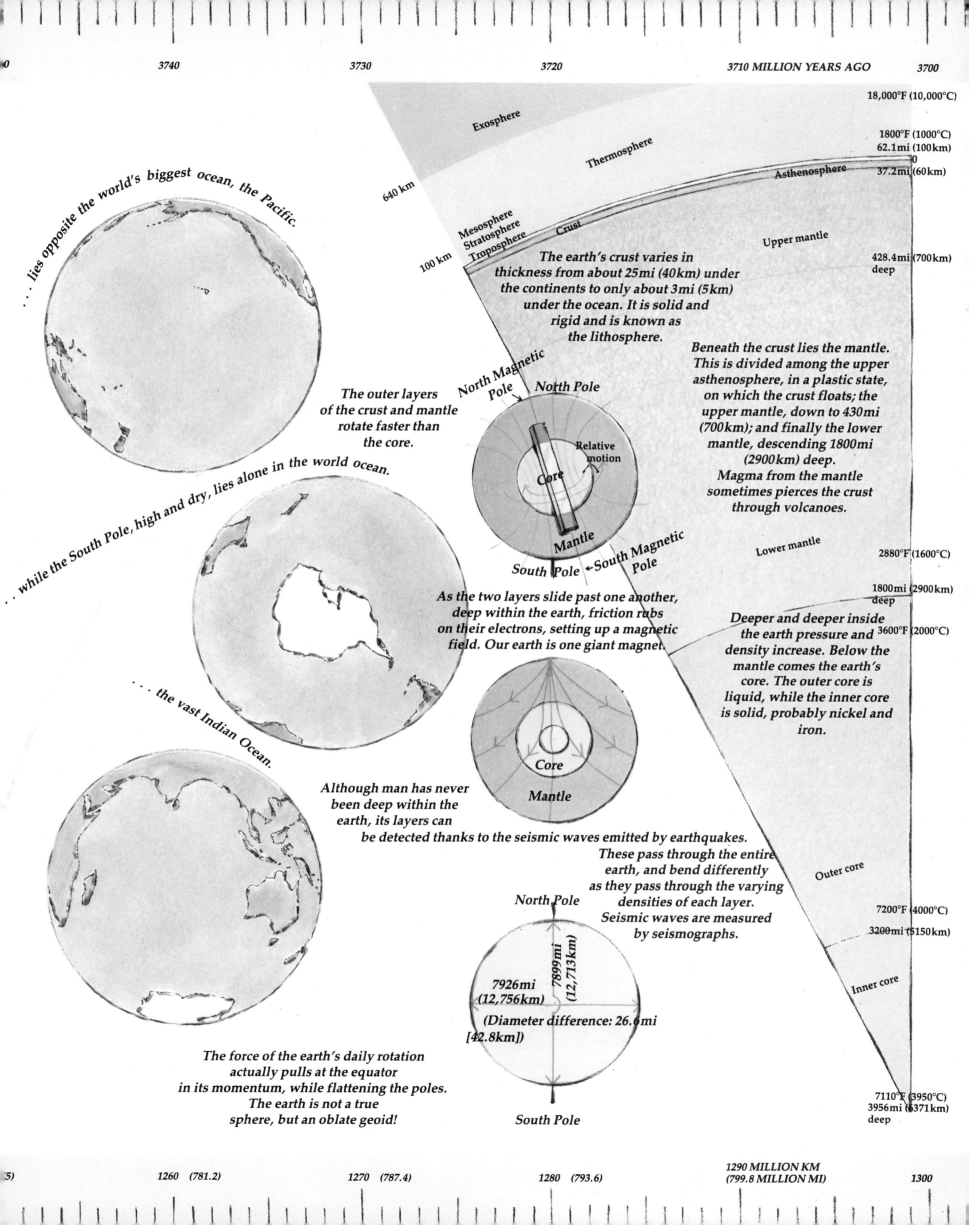

18,000°F (10,000°C)

Exosphere

1800°F (1000°C)
62.1mi (100km)

Thermosphere

Asthenosphere 37.2mi (60km)
0

640 km

Mesosphere
Stratosphere
Troposphere Crust Upper mantle

100 km 428.4mi (700km)
deep

... lies opposite the world's biggest ocean, the Pacific.

The earth's crust varies in
thickness from about 25mi (40km) under
the continents to only about 3mi (5km)
under the ocean. It is solid and
rigid and is known as
the lithosphere.

Beneath the crust lies the mantle.
This is divided among the upper
asthenosphere, in a plastic state,
on which the crust floats; the
upper mantle, down to 430mi
(700km); and finally the lower
mantle, descending 1800mi
(2900km) deep.
Magma from the mantle
sometimes pierces the crust
through volcanoes.

The outer layers
of the crust and mantle
rotate faster than
the core.

North Magnetic
Pole North Pole

Relative
motion

Core

Mantle

South Pole ←South Magnetic
Pole

Lower mantle 2880°F (1600°C)

1800mi (2900km)
deep

Deeper and deeper inside
the earth pressure and 3600°F (2000°C)
density increase. Below the
mantle comes the earth's
core. The outer core is
liquid, while the inner core
is solid, probably nickel and
iron.

... while the South Pole, high and dry, lies alone in the world ocean.

As the two layers slide past one another,
deep within the earth, friction rubs
on their electrons, setting up a magnetic
field. Our earth is one giant magnet.

... the vast Indian Ocean.

Core

Mantle

Although man has never
been deep within the
earth, its layers can
be detected thanks to the seismic waves emitted by earthquakes.
These pass through the entire
earth, and bend differently
as they pass through the varying
densities of each layer.
Seismic waves are measured
by seismographs.

Outer core

North Pole

7926mi
(12,756km)

7899mi
(12,713km)

(Diameter difference: 26.6mi
[42.8km])

7200°F (4000°C)
3200mi (5150km)

Inner core

The force of the earth's daily rotation
actually pulls at the equator
in its momentum, while flattening the poles.
The earth is not a true
sphere, but an oblate geoid!

South Pole

7110°F (3950°C)
3956mi (6371km)
deep

Forces That Build Up

From space the earth's rough surface of mountains and valleys, cliffs and canyons, cannot be seen at all. If a giant could hold the earth in his hand, it would feel as smooth as a glass marble, covered with a thin, damp film . . . the oceans!

Yet tiny as we are on the earth's surface, we are surrounded by a variety of terrain, ranging from mirror-smooth plains to rolling hills and jagged peaks. How did they get there?

There are two distinct forces constantly at work, molding and sculpting the landscape. The first, the mountain-building force, is set to work by the intense heat generated deep within the earth's mantle. This heat wells upward in convection currents, pressing against the fragile crust. The molten magma may force its way up through a crack and reach the surface as a volcano which, as it cools, adds new rock to the earth's surface.

The earth's crust is made up of rock, which over millions of years regenerates itself in a rock cycle. Rocks exposed on the earth's surface are weathered; broken down into small particles by the constant friction of wind and water. These particles are carried by rivers to the sea, where they get deposited as sedimentation. As layers of sediment build up, the lower levels are compressed into sedimentary rock. Sometimes this is pushed by the plates that make up the crust into deep trenches where it melts into molten magma. New surface rock is made from cooling lava ejected from volcanoes.

Mountain chains may be formed when the earth's surface folds under pressure.

Volcano

Lava

If sedimentary rock gets pushed against another crustal plate, bending and buckling under great pressure, the intense heat generated can produce a different type of rock, called metamorphic.

Weathering

Rock particles

transported downstream

Pacific plate

Hot, upwelling magma

A laccolith of cooled lava in a pocket which has raised the rock above.

Sedimentation, compressing into sedimentary rock, in a process called lithification, literally "rock making."

Sedimentary rock pushed down the trench on contact with another crustal plate.

Deep-sea trench

Rock returns to hot, molten magma.

The earth's rocks can be divided into three distinct types:

Igneous rock

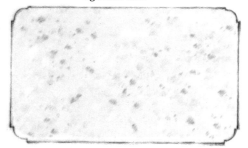

Sedimentary rock

Metamorphic rock

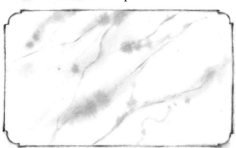

Igneous rock gets its name from the Latin word *ignis*, meaning "fire." Igneous rocks come from molten magma deep within the earth. They surface either by means of volcanoes (extrusive); or through erosion of other overlying rocks (intrusive). Igneous rocks make up about four-fifths of the earth's crust, and they produce excellent agricultural soil. Obsidian, pumice, basalt and granite are some typical igneous rocks.

Sedimentary rock is made up of accumulated material, usually bits of stone, mud and shells, carried by water and deposited on the bottom of lakes and seas in layers. When many layers have accumulated, the bottom ones are pressed together so hard that they cement to become sedimentary rock. This process is called lithification. These rocks form just a thin layer on the earth's surface, but are filled with clues to the earth's past history.
Places where sedimentary rock is found were once underwater, and ancient fossils can be found in them. Sedimentary rocks also hold the world's reserves of gas, oil, coal, salt and groundwater. Shale, clay, sandstone and limestone are examples of sedimentary rock.

Metamorphic rock gets its name from the Greek words meaning "change of form," which is just what happens to igneous or sedimentary rocks which have undergone intense heat and pressure. They turn into metamorphic rock. Two crustal plates pressing on one another may bend sedimentary rocks into new forms. Intense heat may alter the crystal structure of igneous rocks. Metamorphic rocks are found where fold mountains were once built. Some typical examples are gneiss, marble, quartzite and slate.

American plate

American plate

American plate

Eurasian plate

African plate

Eurasian plate

Indo-Australian plate

Pacific plate

Antarctic plate

Many scientists today believe that the earth's crust is made up of separate plates floating on the mantle. When their edges rub against each other we feel it as earthquakes and volcanoes. New crust is formed in the cracks between the plates; while fold mountains are bent upwards under the pressure of two bumping plates. Old crust returns to the mantle via deep trenches between the plates.

The earth's continental crustal plates fit on the earth's surface like the patchwork of a quilt.

Strike-slip fault

Block mountain (Horst)

Anticline

Syncline

Thrust

Rift valley (Graben)

Chains of mountains are formed either by the folding of the earth's crust under pressure; or by the slippage of whole blocks of crust along faults.
Although such up-lifting processes are called mountain-building processes, mountains are also sculpted by erosion, as we shall see.

The earth's crust is actually believed to float on the denser, but molten, mantle like a scum of cream on the surface of a bowl of milk. The crust is broken into several pieces, or plates, which we also call continents. A plate of crust may be pushed aside by welling-up magma, or by friction against another plate, causing an earthquake. Over longer periods of time, the magma may bend and buckle the plate skywards to form mountain ranges.

Were this mountain-building force to go unchecked, the earth's surface might resemble that of the moon. But all the time the earth is building itself up, another force is busily breaking it down! We call this force the weathering force or, more simply, erosion.

33

Forces That Break Down

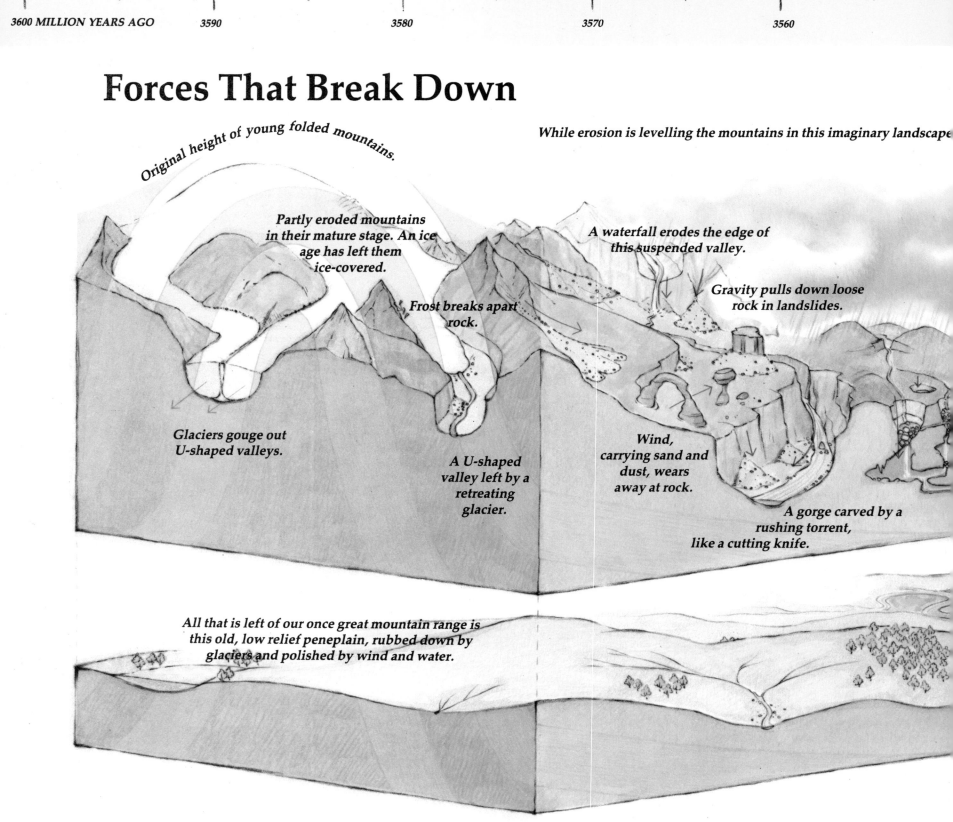

Original height of young folded mountains.

While erosion is levelling the mountains in this imaginary landscape

Partly eroded mountains in their mature stage. An ice age has left them ice-covered.

A waterfall erodes the edge of this suspended valley.

Gravity pulls down loose rock in landslides.

Frost breaks apart rock.

Glaciers gouge out U-shaped valleys.

A U-shaped valley left by a retreating glacier.

Wind, carrying sand and dust, wears away at rock.

A gorge carved by a rushing torrent, like a cutting knife.

All that is left of our once great mountain range is this old, low relief peneplain, rubbed down by glaciers and polished by wind and water.

During a cold, icy winter, you have perhaps seen the roads' surface crack and break. In summer, by the sea, standing barefoot by the wet shore, you may have noticed how the waves pull the sand from beneath your feet. You have probably seen old paint flake off housefronts; or how cars, or wood, when left in the rain, will rust or rot. You are witnessing the weathering force!

34   The earth is one of the few planets in the

solar system with an atmosphere, and perhaps the only one with water. A planet like the moon has little or no weathering, or erosion, since there is no wind or water to wear things down. Planet earth, however, because of its atmosphere, its tilt (varying seasons), and its frequent day and night cycle (heat and frost), has wind and weather to rub and grind down the surface.

Because the earth has vast reserves of

the mountain-building process is busy making new ones elsewhere!

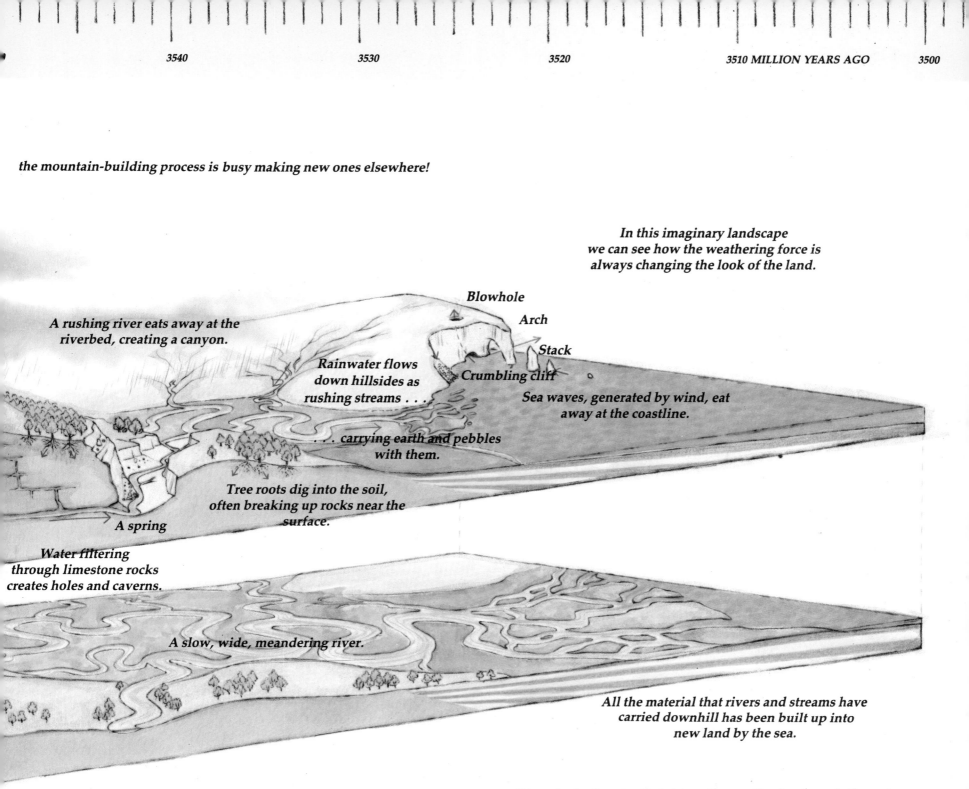

*In this imaginary landscape
we can see how the weathering force is
always changing the look of the land.*

Blowhole

Arch

Stack

*A rushing river eats away at the
riverbed, creating a canyon.*

**Rainwater flows
down hillsides as
rushing streams . . .**

Crumbling cliff

*Sea waves, generated by wind, eat
away at the coastline.*

*. . . carrying earth and pebbles
with them.*

**Tree roots dig into the soil,
often breaking up rocks near the
surface.**

A spring

**Water filtering
through limestone rocks
creates holes and caverns.**

A slow, wide, meandering river.

*All the material that rivers and streams have
carried downhill has been built up into
new land by the sea.*

*The principal motor that drives the weathering force is the water
cycle, running on sunlight (causing evaporation) and gravity.*

water and a good gravity force there is rain and snow. The water provides rushing streams and waterfalls to cut out valleys and canyons, and rivers to carry the gouged stone and mud elsewhere.

The forces of erosion work like a great polishing stone, wearing the planet's face smooth. Why, if erosion had all its own way, it would level the earth's surface absolutely flat!

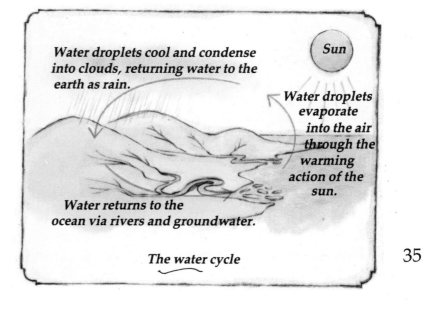

Sun

*Water droplets cool and condense
into clouds, returning water to the
earth as rain.*

*Water droplets
evaporate
into the air
through the
warming
action of the
sun.*

*Water returns to the
ocean via rivers and groundwater.*

The water cycle

35

Earth's Changing Face

It is fun to look at old photos. You probably have some pictures of yourself when you were a baby. It's hard to believe that the baby is really you, the face looks so different! How will it compare with a picture of you in sixty years, all gray hair and wrinkles? It is hard to believe that the different faces belong to the same person.

Just as people's faces change with age, so does the earth's. If we had a photo of our planet several million years old, we would have a hard time recognizing where we live.

The continents would have unfamiliar shapes, the oceans would be in different places and some of the great mountain chains might not appear at all! Similarly, a photo of our planet in the future would be equally surprising, for the mountains we ski on today will have been eroded flat, and the continents will have moved to new positions. For as we have seen, the earth is in a constant state of change from the two great forces that are right now building it up, and breaking it down.

As we go through life we are constantly changing. Our cells regenerate and our bone structure develops continuously. The change is relatively slow so that we don't see the changes from day to day, but only after several years.

Continental shelf

Eurasian plate

American plate

Pacific plate

African plate

Indo-Australian plate

Pacific plate

Continental shelf

Antarctic plate

The earth's structure is also changing, but its life is so much longer that we can see the differences only after thousands of years. The earth's crust is made up of a number of plates which are floating on the molten mantle beneath, like blocks of ice on water.

Convection currents in the mantle may force the plates to shift on the earth's surface, moving the continents with them. The earth's face is constantly changing (over great spans of time), through this process called continental drift.

Coastlines do not form the real edges of the continents, any more than a waterline shows the bottom of a boat: their real bottom is under water! Continents have their true edges on their continental shelves, often many miles out to sea.

Recent exploration of the oceans has shown that the sea floor is much thinner and much newer than the rock beneath the continents. Great chains of active volcanoes have also been found running along the ocean floors. Many scientists now believe that new crust is being created by these submerged volcanoes, and that they are actually pushing apart the existing crustal plates, in a process called sea-floor spreading. As the crustal plates move apart, the continents move too, floating on an ocean of magma beneath. This idea of moving continents is known as the theory of continental drift.

If new crust is being formed beneath the sea, and the crustal plates are spreading, then what is happening at their opposite edges? The opposite edges quite simply bump together, folding the crust up into mountains, or folding it down to return to the molten mantle. However, sometimes the strain on a plate will become so great that it breaks violently, and then we feel an earthquake.

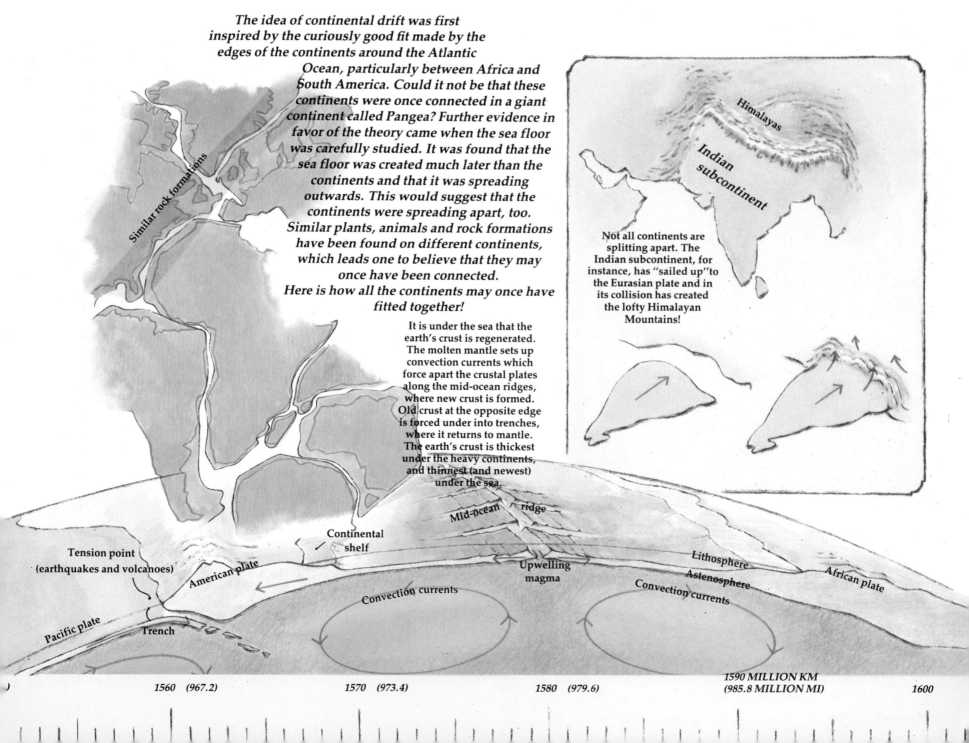

The idea of continental drift was first inspired by the curiously good fit made by the edges of the continents around the Atlantic Ocean, particularly between Africa and South America. Could it not be that these continents were once connected in a giant continent called Pangea? Further evidence in favor of the theory came when the sea floor was carefully studied. It was found that the sea floor was created much later than the continents and that it was spreading outwards. This would suggest that the continents were spreading apart, too. Similar plants, animals and rock formations have been found on different continents, which leads one to believe that they may once have been connected.
Here is how all the continents may once have fitted together!

Similar rock formations

It is under the sea that the earth's crust is regenerated. The molten mantle sets up convection currents which force apart the crustal plates along the mid-ocean ridges, where new crust is formed. Old crust at the opposite edge is forced under into trenches, where it returns to mantle. The earth's crust is thickest under the heavy continents, and thinnest (and newest) under the sea.

Himalayas

Indian subcontinent

Not all continents are splitting apart. The Indian subcontinent, for instance, has "sailed up" to the Eurasian plate and in its collision has created the lofty Himalayan Mountains!

Tension point (earthquakes and volcanoes)

Continental shelf

Mid-ocean ridge

Upwelling magma

Lithosphere

Astenosphere

African plate

American plate

Convection currents

Convection currents

Pacific plate

Trench

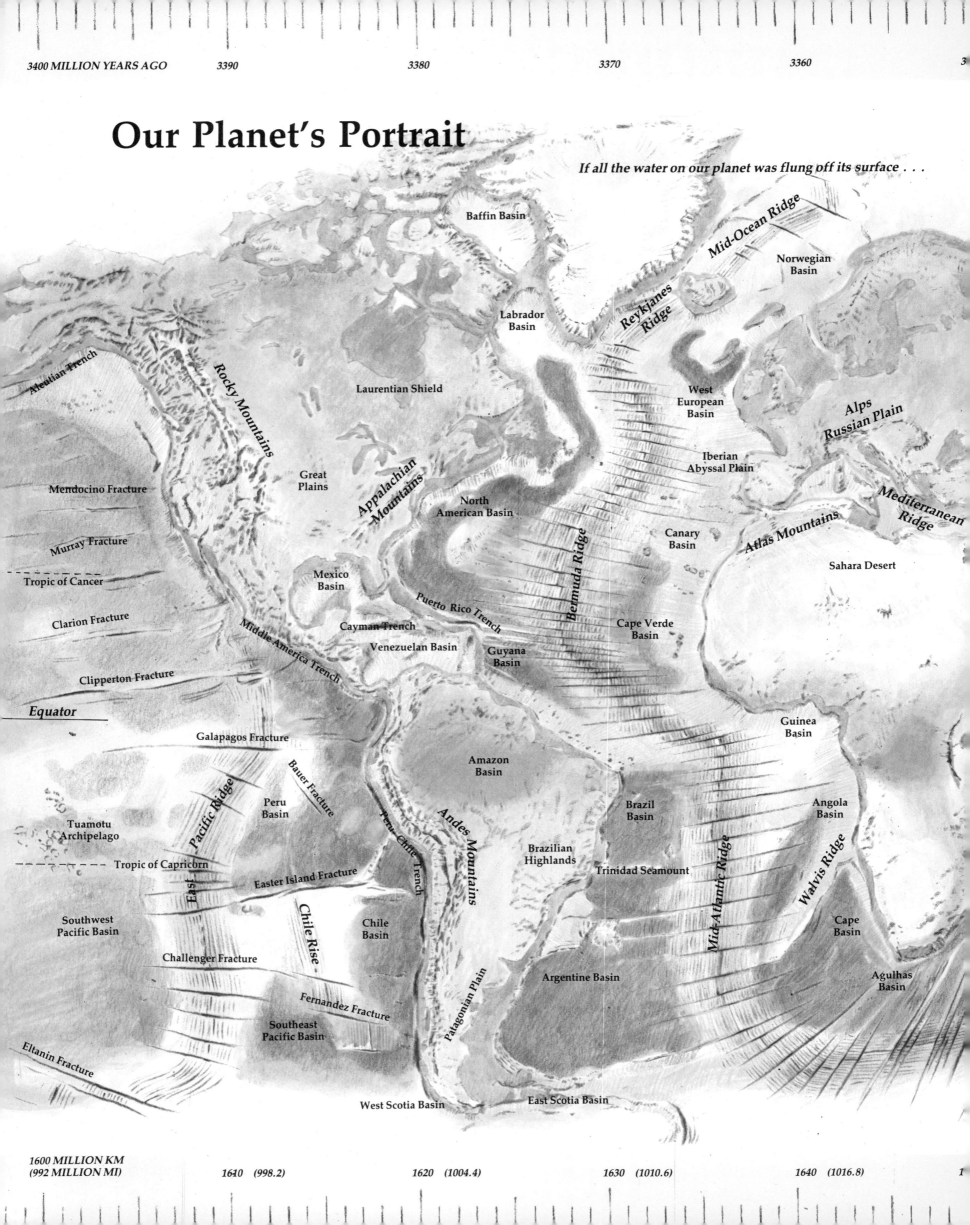

Our Planet's Portrait

If all the water on our planet was flung off its surface . . .

Baffin Basin

Mid-Ocean Ridge

Norwegian Basin

Labrador Basin

Reykjanes Ridge

Aleutian Trench

Rocky Mountains

Laurentian Shield

West European Basin

Alps

Russian Plain

Mendocino Fracture

Great Plains

Appalachian Mountains

North American Basin

Iberian Abyssal Plain

Mediterranean Ridge

Murray Fracture

Canary Basin

Atlas Mountains

Tropic of Cancer

Mexico Basin

Sahara Desert

Clarion Fracture

Puerto Rico Trench

Bermuda Ridge

Cape Verde Basin

Cayman Trench

Middle America Trench

Venezuelan Basin

Guyana Basin

Clipperton Fracture

Equator

Guinea Basin

Galapagos Fracture

Amazon Basin

Bauer Fracture

Brazil Basin

Angola Basin

Peru Basin

East Pacific Ridge

Peru-Chile Trench

Andes Mountains

Tuamotu Archipelago

Brazilian Highlands

Mid-Atlantic Ridge

Walvis Ridge

Tropic of Capricorn

Easter Island Fracture

Trinidad Seamount

Southwest Pacific Basin

Chile Rise

Chile Basin

Cape Basin

Challenger Fracture

Fernandez Fracture

Argentine Basin

Agulhas Basin

Southeast Pacific Basin

Patagonian Plain

Eltanin Fracture

West Scotia Basin

East Scotia Basin

. . . here is what we'd see!   Compare this "earth-scape" with that of the moon on page 26.

Ural Mountains

Siberian Plain

Central Siberian Plateau

Aleutian Basin

Kuril Basin

Emperor Seamount Chain

Gobi Desert

Japan Basin

Tarim Basin

Plateau of Tibet

Syrian Desert

Plateau of Iran

Himalayan Mountains

Great Plain of China

Mid-Pacific Mountains

Arabian Peninsula

Red Sea Rift

Arabian Basin

Ganges Fan

Philippine Basin

South China Basin

Tropic of Cancer

Rift Valley

Somali Basin

Andman Basin

Celebes Basin

East Caroline Basin

Carlsberg Ridge

Cocos Basin

Equator

Madagascar Basin

Mid-Indian Basin

Java Trench

Coral Sea Basin

New Hebrides Trench

Tonga Trench

Rodriguez Fracture

Wharton Basin

Ninety East Ridge

Natal Basin

West Australian Basin

Great Sandy Desert

Great Dividing Range

Lord Home Rise

Tropic of Capricorn

Mozambic Fracture

Southwest Indian Ridge

Mid-Indian Ridge

South Indian Basin

Broken Ridge

Great Victoria Desert

South Australian Basin

Tasman Basin

Kermadec Trench

Atlantic-Indian Ridge

Diamantina Fracture

Bounty Trench

Southeast Indian Ridge

Tasman Ridge

Atlantic-Indian Basin

Earth's Protective Overcoat

Our existence on earth is rather like living at the bottom of a big ocean. We crawl about on its floor like little crabs, and airplanes and birds dart through it like fish in water. We scarcely feel this "ocean's" presence, and rarely even see it, but without it we could not live. We call it the atmosphere.

The atmosphere is made up of a mixture of gases. Several other planets also have an atmosphere, but only earth's has just the right gases to permit life: oxygen, nitrogen, carbon dioxide and water vapor.

Like real oceans, the atmosphere has weight and pressure. Held down by the earth's gravity, it is densest at the bottom . . . the earth's surface.

Our atmosphere also acts as a protective shield, filtering out many harmful light rays from the sun. And, like a duck's eiderdown, it helps retain the sun's warmth during the hours of night. The atmosphere also protects the earth's surface from being hit by interplanetary matter, for friction against it burns up any such matter.

The mixture of gases in the atmosphere, which we call air, carries dust and water droplets. These, in the form of clouds, carry water all over the earth's surface, allowing plants to grow.

When the earth was newly formed the atmosphere around it condensed, forming water. Centuries of rain filled most of the planet's surface and gave us the deep, blue seas which became the cradle of life on earth.

40

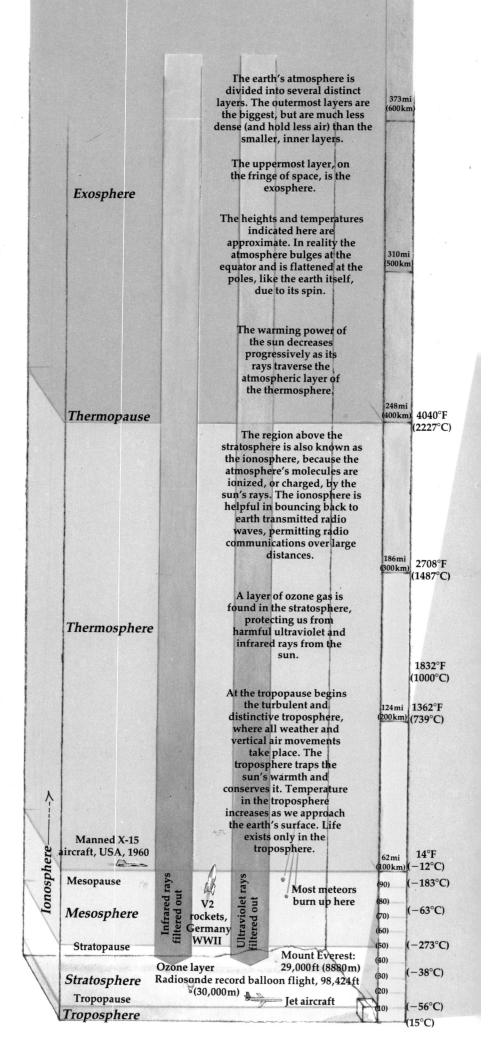

The earth's atmosphere is divided into several distinct layers. The outermost layers are the biggest, but are much less dense (and hold less air) than the smaller, inner layers.

The uppermost layer, on the fringe of space, is the exosphere.

The heights and temperatures indicated here are approximate. In reality the atmosphere bulges at the equator and is flattened at the poles, like the earth itself, due to its spin.

The warming power of the sun decreases progressively as its rays traverse the atmospheric layer of the thermosphere.

The region above the stratosphere is also known as the ionosphere, because the atmosphere's molecules are ionized, or charged, by the sun's rays. The ionosphere is helpful in bouncing back to earth transmitted radio waves, permitting radio communications over large distances.

A layer of ozone gas is found in the stratosphere, protecting us from harmful ultraviolet and infrared rays from the sun.

At the tropopause begins the turbulent and distinctive troposphere, where all weather and vertical air movements take place. The troposphere traps the sun's warmth and conserves it. Temperature in the troposphere increases as we approach the earth's surface. Life exists only in the troposphere.

Exosphere

Thermopause

Thermosphere

Ionosphere ———→

Mesopause

Mesosphere

Stratopause

Stratosphere

Tropopause

Troposphere

Manned X-15 aircraft, USA, 1960

Infrared rays filtered out

V2 rockets, Germany WWII

Ultraviolet rays filtered out

Most meteors burn up here

Ozone layer

Mount Everest: 29,000ft (8880m)

Radiosonde record balloon flight, 98,424ft (30,000m)

Jet aircraft

373mi (600km)

310mi (500km)

248mi (400km)   4040°F (2227°C)

186mi (300km)   2708°F (1487°C)

1832°F (1000°C)

124mi (200km)   1362°F (739°C)

62mi (100km)   14°F (−12°C)

(90)   (−183°C)
(80)
(70)   (−63°C)
(60)
(50)   (−273°C)
(40)
(30)   (−38°C)
(20)
(10)   (−56°C)
    (15°C)

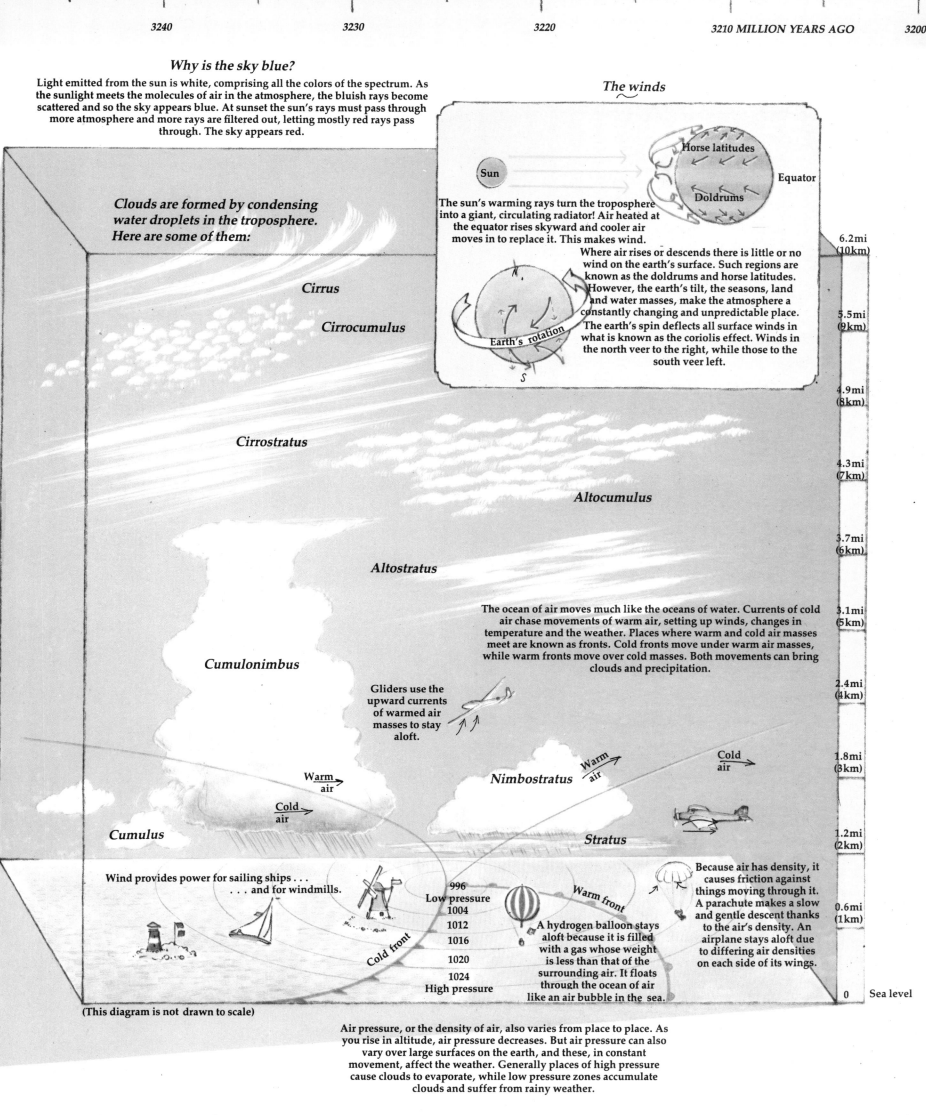

Why is the sky blue?

Light emitted from the sun is white, comprising all the colors of the spectrum. As the sunlight meets the molecules of air in the atmosphere, the bluish rays become scattered and so the sky appears blue. At sunset the sun's rays must pass through more atmosphere and more rays are filtered out, letting mostly red rays pass through. The sky appears red.

Clouds are formed by condensing water droplets in the troposphere. Here are some of them:

Cirrus

Cirrocumulus

Cirrostratus

Altocumulus

Altostratus

Cumulonimbus

Cumulus

Nimbostratus

Stratus

The winds

Sun   Horse latitudes   Equator   Doldrums

The sun's warming rays turn the troposphere into a giant, circulating radiator! Air heated at the equator rises skyward and cooler air moves in to replace it. This makes wind.

Where air rises or descends there is little or no wind on the earth's surface. Such regions are known as the doldrums and horse latitudes. However, the earth's tilt, the seasons, land and water masses, make the atmosphere a constantly changing and unpredictable place.

The earth's spin deflects all surface winds in what is known as the coriolis effect. Winds in the north veer to the right, while those to the south veer left.

Earth's rotation   N   S

The ocean of air moves much like the oceans of water. Currents of cold air chase movements of warm air, setting up winds, changes in temperature and the weather. Places where warm and cold air masses meet are known as fronts. Cold fronts move under warm air masses, while warm fronts move over cold masses. Both movements can bring clouds and precipitation.

Gliders use the upward currents of warmed air masses to stay aloft.

Warm air

Cold air

Warm air

Cold air

Wind provides power for sailing ships . . .
. . . and for windmills.

Because air has density, it causes friction against things moving through it. A parachute makes a slow and gentle descent thanks to the air's density. An airplane stays aloft due to differing air densities on each side of its wings.

996 Low pressure
1004
1012
1016
1020
1024 High pressure

Warm front

Cold front

A hydrogen balloon stays aloft because it is filled with a gas whose weight is less than that of the surrounding air. It floats through the ocean of air like an air bubble in the sea.

(This diagram is not drawn to scale)

Air pressure, or the density of air, also varies from place to place. As you rise in altitude, air pressure decreases. But air pressure can also vary over large surfaces on the earth, and these, in constant movement, affect the weather. Generally places of high pressure cause clouds to evaporate, while low pressure zones accumulate clouds and suffer from rainy weather.

6.2mi (10km)
5.5mi (9km)
4.9mi (8km)
4.3mi (7km)
3.7mi (6km)
3.1mi (5km)
2.4mi (4km)
1.8mi (3km)
1.2mi (2km)
0.6mi (1km)
0   Sea level

Planet Ocean

For most of us, in our minds, the earth is land. Many of us have never seen the ocean, and most have only seen its shore. From land our view of the earth is far from complete. Indeed, from space we can see that the continents are but islands floating on a planet of water. In fact the oceans, or more correctly *the* world ocean, covers a good 70 percent of our planet. We might be tempted to rename our planet earth, planet ocean!

The ocean has always been a mysterious place. Even today more is probably known about the surface of the moon than the depths of our own planet.

In the past the ocean was seen by man as a terrifying barrier, blocking his route to distant shores. Fishing its waters was a perilous business reserved only for the brave or foolhardy.

Today we are just beginning to change that idea. The vast ocean, rich in life and resources, may be man's only salvation to continue living on an overcrowded earth.

In its infant years the earth bore little resemblance to the one we know today. The atmosphere was a poisonous gas, and the unfiltered sunrays made life intolerable on the earth's surface. It was under the protective blanket of water that the first micro-organisms flourished. Feeding on water and sunlight, through a process called photosynthesis, these micro-plants emitted oxygen into the atmosphere. After millions of years the atmosphere took on a more familiar composition, and the first plants were able to poke their heads above water and eventually take root on land.

Animals, which had developed exclusively in the sea, followed. Perhaps the first animals to put their nose on a beach did so to lay their eggs there, safe from predators. With food available on land, in the form of plants, animals adapted to spend more and more time out of their original element, the sea.

We, as human beings, the last link in the chain of evolution, have lost all contact with the sea. For generations we have dumped our waste there and have been fishing its inhabitants to extinction. Yet the sea is our birthplace, and it is fitting that in this era of dwindling land resources man is seeking his future in the sea.

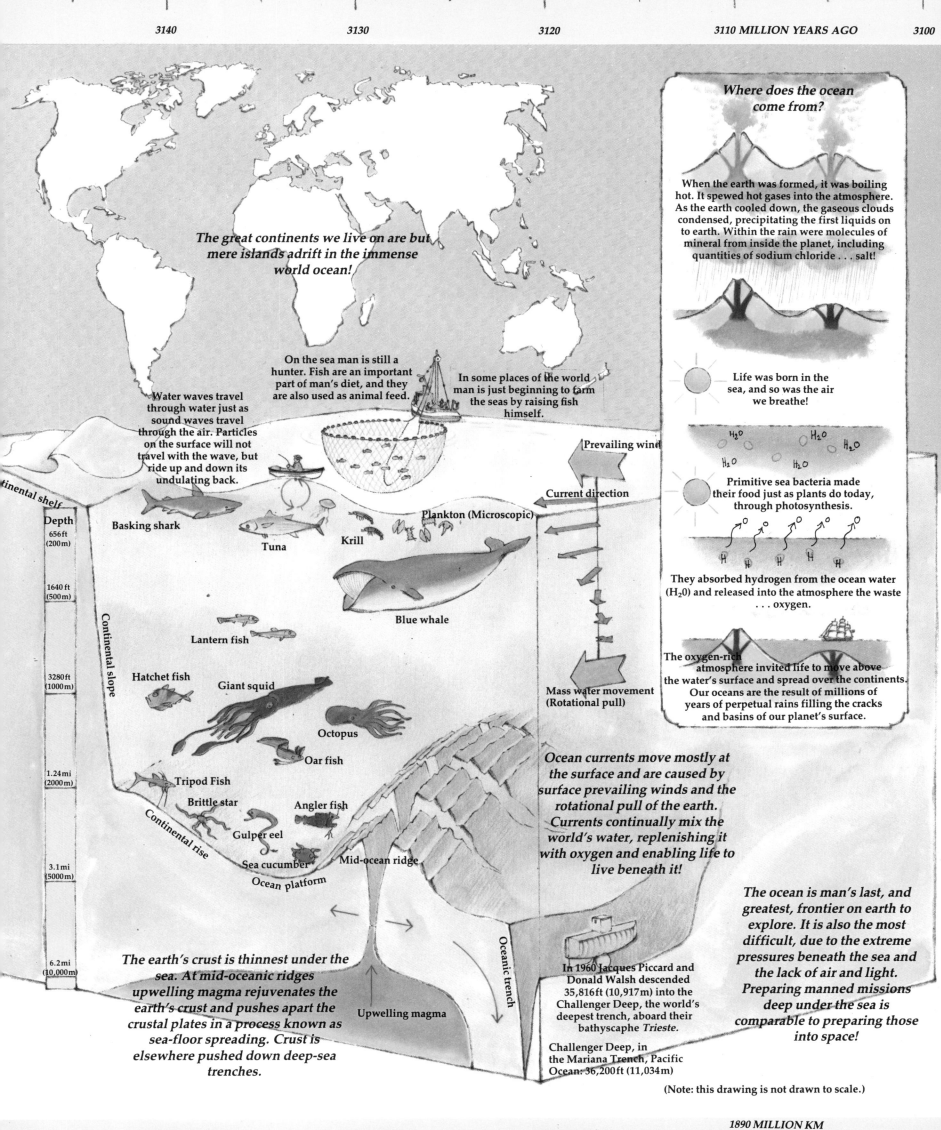

The great continents we live on are but mere islands adrift in the immense world ocean!

Where does the ocean come from?

When the earth was formed, it was boiling hot. It spewed hot gases into the atmosphere. As the earth cooled down, the gaseous clouds condensed, precipitating the first liquids on to earth. Within the rain were molecules of mineral from inside the planet, including quantities of sodium chloride . . . salt!

Life was born in the sea, and so was the air we breathe!

H_2O H_2O H_2O H_2O H_2O

Primitive sea bacteria made their food just as plants do today, through photosynthesis.

They absorbed hydrogen from the ocean water (H_2O) and released into the atmosphere the waste . . . oxygen.

The oxygen-rich atmosphere invited life to move above the water's surface and spread over the continents. Our oceans are the result of millions of years of perpetual rains filling the cracks and basins of our planet's surface.

On the sea man is still a hunter. Fish are an important part of man's diet, and they are also used as animal feed.

In some places of the world man is just beginning to farm the seas by raising fish himself.

Water waves travel through water just as sound waves travel through the air. Particles on the surface will not travel with the wave, but ride up and down its undulating back.

Prevailing wind

Current direction

Plankton (Microscopic)

Continental shelf

Depth

656 ft (200m)

Basking shark

Tuna

Krill

1640 ft (500m)

Continental slope

Blue whale

Lantern fish

3280 ft (1000m)

Hatchet fish

Giant squid

Octopus

Oar fish

Mass water movement (Rotational pull)

1.24 mi (2000m)

Tripod Fish

Brittle star

Angler fish

Gulper eel

Continental rise

Sea cucumber

Mid-ocean ridge

Ocean platform

3.1 mi (5000m)

Ocean currents move mostly at the surface and are caused by surface prevailing winds and the rotational pull of the earth. Currents continually mix the world's water, replenishing it with oxygen and enabling life to live beneath it!

The ocean is man's last, and greatest, frontier on earth to explore. It is also the most difficult, due to the extreme pressures beneath the sea and the lack of air and light. Preparing manned missions deep under the sea is comparable to preparing those into space!

6.2 mi (10,000m)

The earth's crust is thinnest under the sea. At mid-oceanic ridges upwelling magma rejuvenates the earth's crust and pushes apart the crustal plates in a process known as sea-floor spreading. Crust is elsewhere pushed down deep-sea trenches.

Upwelling magma

Oceanic trench

In 1960 Jacques Piccard and Donald Walsh descended 35,816 ft (10,917m) into the Challenger Deep, the world's deepest trench, aboard their bathyscaphe *Trieste*.

Challenger Deep, in the Mariana Trench, Pacific Ocean: 36,200 ft (11,034m)

(Note: this drawing is not drawn to scale.)

The Bricks of Life

If you were asked "Just *what* is a living thing?" would you know the answer? You might say that a living thing breathes. Yes, but so does a bellows, and that is not alive. Living things move, but so do non-living things, like cars. Living things grow, but crystals, non-living, can grow too, adding new layers to themselves. There is just one thing that non-living things cannot do, and that is to reproduce. Everything that is alive, be it you, your dog, a flower or a tree, has the ability to make replicas of itself, or offspring.

Everything alive is made up of millions upon millions of tiny, living cells. Cells are the bricks, or building-blocks, of living things. Cells can reproduce too, by splitting themselves in two. If you stumble and scrape your knee, your skin cells will get to work to reproduce the damaged skin and repair the wound.

You may wonder, as scientists have wondered for years, who tells the cells when and what to do? Scientists have recently discovered a marvelous microscopic molecule, located deep within the cells. These molecules, called DNA, are made like long,

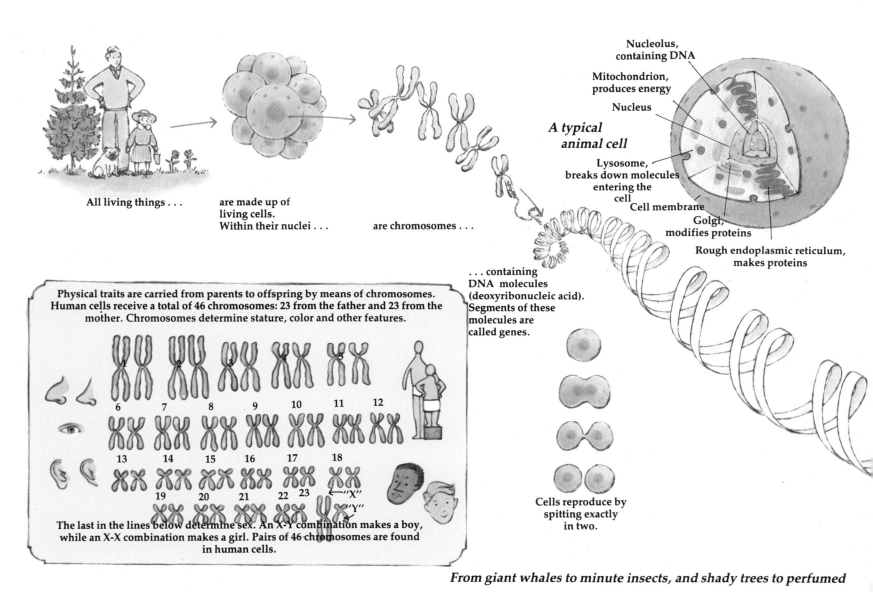

All living things . . .

are made up of living cells. Within their nuclei . . .

are chromosomes . . .

A typical animal cell

Nucleolus, containing DNA

Mitochondrion, produces energy

Nucleus

Lysosome, breaks down molecules entering the cell

Cell membrane

Golgi, modifies proteins

Rough endoplasmic reticulum, makes proteins

. . . containing DNA molecules (deoxyribonucleic acid). Segments of these molecules are called genes.

Physical traits are carried from parents to offspring by means of chromosomes. Human cells receive a total of 46 chromosomes: 23 from the father and 23 from the mother. Chromosomes determine stature, color and other features.

1   2   3   4   5

6   7   8   9   10   11   12

13   14   15   16   17   18

19   20   21   22   23   ←"X" ←"Y"

The last in the lines below determine sex. An X-Y combination makes a boy, while an X-X combination makes a girl. Pairs of 46 chromosomes are found in human cells.

Cells reproduce by spitting exactly in two.

44

From giant whales to minute insects, and shady trees to perfumed

twisted ladders, and on each rung are the instructions for the cell to follow. Scientists are fascinated with DNA molecules because they are the ultimate "grains of life," and control of them might heal man's illnesses.

When the cells of a living thing split, to produce offspring, they usually reproduce exact copies of themselves. Sometimes, however, they might accidentally make offspring not quite faithful to the original. The offspring might have a deficiency – lacking a finger, for instance. But sometimes, very rarely, it might make the offspring even better suited for life. Such modifications in offspring are called mutations.

As the earth itself has changed through the ages, so have living things adapted to those changes. The changes have been gradual, over many generations. We are the result of innumerable mutations, stemming from apes, which permit us to live in almost any part of the globe. Through mutations in offspring nature selects those best suited for life. Thus, as the earth has evolved, so have the living things. That is the story of evolution through natural selection.

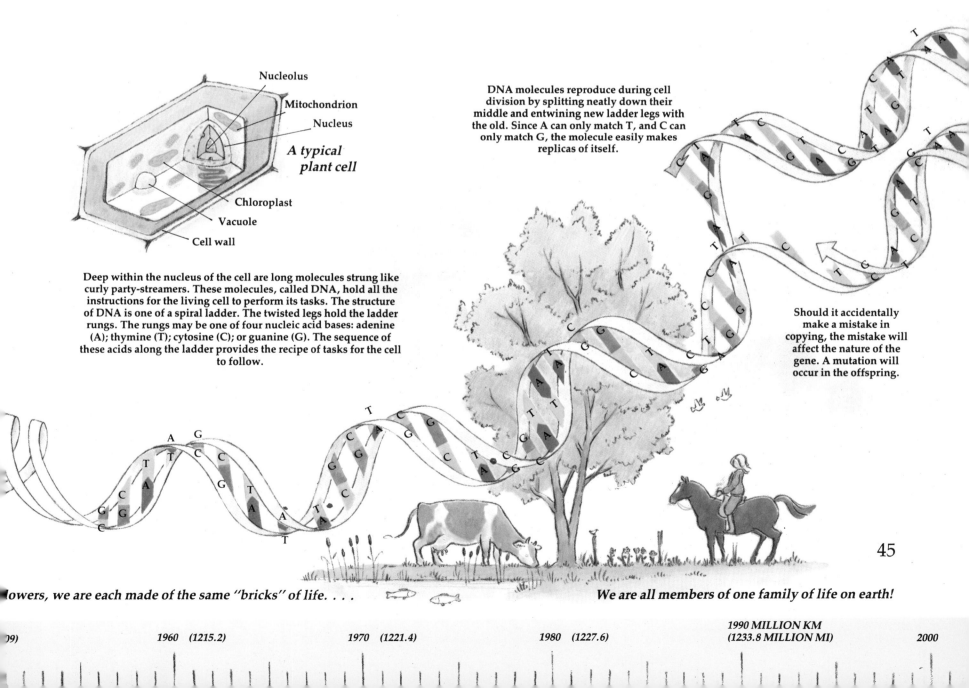

Nucleolus

Mitochondrion

Nucleus

A typical plant cell

Chloroplast

Vacuole

Cell wall

Deep within the nucleus of the cell are long molecules strung like curly party-streamers. These molecules, called DNA, hold all the instructions for the living cell to perform its tasks. The structure of DNA is one of a spiral ladder. The twisted legs hold the ladder rungs. The rungs may be one of four nucleic acid bases: adenine (A); thymine (T); cytosine (C); or guanine (G). The sequence of these acids along the ladder provides the recipe of tasks for the cell to follow.

DNA molecules reproduce during cell division by splitting neatly down their middle and entwining new ladder legs with the old. Since A can only match T, and C can only match G, the molecule easily makes replicas of itself.

Should it accidentally make a mistake in copying, the mistake will affect the nature of the gene. A mutation will occur in the offspring.

45

...owers, we are each made of the same "bricks" of life. . . .   *We are all members of one family of life on earth!*

The Family Tree of Life

The Old Testament of the Bible states that God created the earth in just six days. He made the oceans one day, the mountains on another, all the plants and animals, and on the sixth day man himself. After all that work, he took the seventh day to rest. For hundreds of years people believed this was how the earth was made, and all its inhabitants created.

We know now that the earth has been going through perpetual change. Its once poisonous atmosphere became a supporter of life; its continents shifted, tore apart, or bumped together. It has gone through periods of intense cold, when the oceans became locked in ice. No animals on earth today could have endured such drastic changes in climate, so could it not be that animals changed, or adapted themselves to suit the changes of the earth? This is the question that a young English naturalist aboard a sailing ship in the tropical seas asked himself. His name was Charles Darwin.

Coming from the temperate climate of England, Darwin was impressed by the profusion of life forms in the tropics. He found dozens of varieties of the same type of animal: tortoises with slightly different shells; or birds with slightly different beaks, depending on where they lived and what they found to eat. Would God have made so

The forearms of different species show similarities in structure, but each is adapted to a particular function, be it lifting, propelling through the air, or through water. The theory of evolution believes arm type has adapted to meet different necessities.

Bird wing

Human arm

Bat wing

Turtle arm (reptile)

Single-celled life

Algae

Lichens

Fungi

Mosses

Horsetails

Club mosses

Bacteria

Ferns

Cycads

Conifers

Flowering plants

Quaternary

Cenozoic era   *Mesozoic era*   *Paleozoic era*

Tertiary period

Cretaceous

Jurassic

Triassic

Permian

Carboniferous

0 | 5 | 64 | 136 | 195 | 225 | 280 | 345

many endless varieties of animal to inhabit the earth? Could it be that nature had adapted the animals over generations to survive where they lived?

After returning to England, and after

46

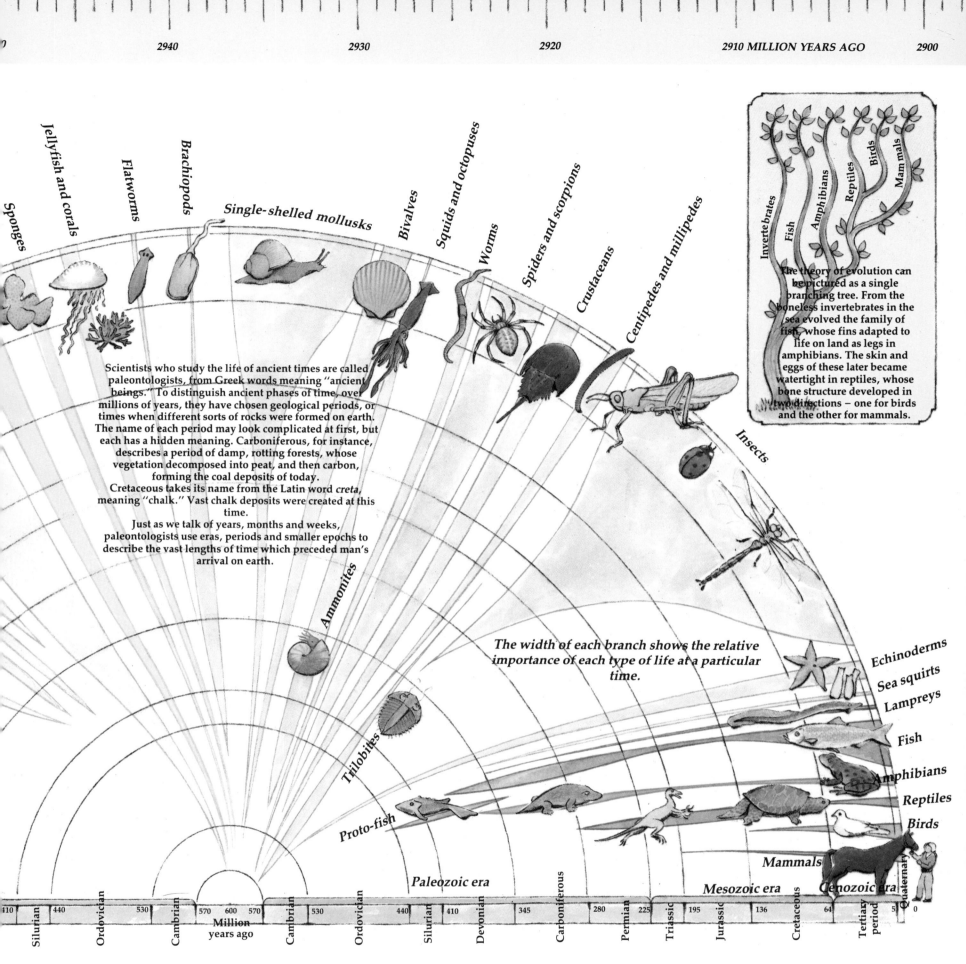

Sponges

Jellyfish and corals

Flatworms

Brachiopods

Single-shelled mollusks

Bivalves

Squids and octopuses

Worms

Spiders and scorpions

Crustaceans

Centipedes and millipedes

Invertebrates · Fish · Amphibians · Reptiles · Birds · Mammals

The theory of evolution can be pictured as a single branching tree. From the boneless invertebrates in the sea evolved the family of fish, whose fins adapted to life on land as legs in amphibians. The skin and eggs of these later became watertight in reptiles, whose bone structure developed in two directions – one for birds and the other for mammals.

Insects

Scientists who study the life of ancient times are called paleontologists, from Greek words meaning "ancient beings." To distinguish ancient phases of time, over millions of years, they have chosen geological periods, or times when different sorts of rocks were formed on earth. The name of each period may look complicated at first, but each has a hidden meaning. Carboniferous, for instance, describes a period of damp, rotting forests, whose vegetation decomposed into peat, and then carbon, forming the coal deposits of today.
Cretaceous takes its name from the Latin word *creta*, meaning "chalk." Vast chalk deposits were created at this time.
Just as we talk of years, months and weeks, paleontologists use eras, periods and smaller epochs to describe the vast lengths of time which preceded man's arrival on earth.

Ammonites

The width of each branch shows the relative importance of each type of life at a particular time.

Echinoderms

Sea squirts

Lampreys

Fish

Amphibians

Reptiles

Birds

Mammals

Trilobites

Proto-fish

Paleozoic era

Mesozoic era

Cenozoic era

Silurian 410 · 440 Ordovician · 530 Cambrian · 570 600 570 Million years ago · Cambrian · 530 Ordovician · 440 Silurian · 410 Devonian · 345 Carboniferous · 280 Permian · 225 Triassic · 195 Jurassic · 136 Cretaceous · 64 Tertiary period · 5 Quaternary · 0

years of hesitation, Darwin published his ideas on evolution. Everyone ridiculed his theories, which related man himself to the apes!

Since then we have learned that the variety of life, from microbes to plants, through fish, reptiles, birds and mammals, is a chain of innumerable mutations in heredity to enable life to cope with the ever-changing earth.

47

From the Roots of Life . . .

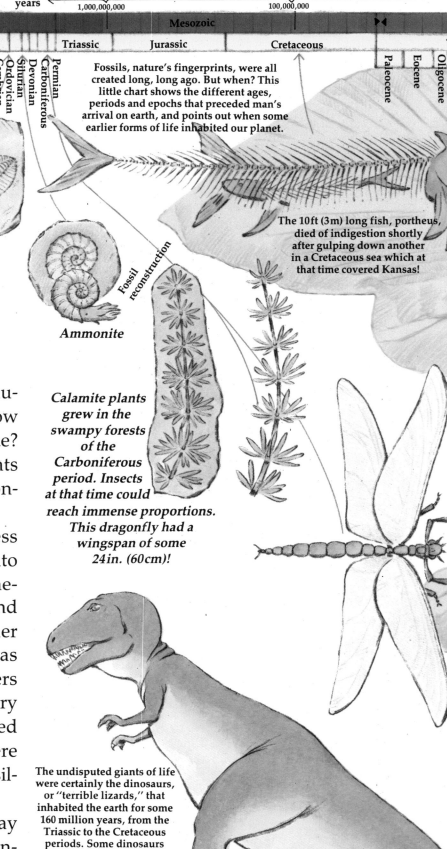

Nine billion years ← Nine-hundred million years   Ninety million years

1,000,000,000   100,000,000   10,000,000

Paleozoic   Mesozoic

Pre-Cambrian
Cambrian
Ordovician
Silurian
Devonian
Carboniferous
Permian

Triassic   Jurassic   Cretaceous   Tertiary

Paleocene
Eocene
Oligocene
Miocene

Fossils, nature's fingerprints, were all created long, long ago. But when? This little chart shows the different ages, periods and epochs that preceded man's arrival on earth, and points out when some earlier forms of life inhabited our planet.

Trilobites and ammonites were animals that lived in the primitive seas of the Cambrian and Ordovician periods. Jellyfish existed already since Pre-Cambrian times, but their soft, boneless bodies have left us no fossils.

Trilobite

Fossil reconstruction

Ammonite

The 10ft (3m) long fish, portheus, died of indigestion shortly after gulping down another in a Cretaceous sea which at that time covered Kansas!

Calamite plants grew in the swampy forests of the Carboniferous period. Insects at that time could reach immense proportions. This dragonfly had a wingspan of some 24in. (60cm)!

How do paleontologists know that evolution has taken place? How do they know what extinct plants and animals looked like? Just as a careless burglar leaves fingerprints for a detective, nature has provided paleontologists with fossils.

On pages 34–5 we saw that in the process of erosion fine rock particles are carried into the sea, where they form sediment. Sometimes plants or animals fall into the sea, and just rarely they may be quickly buried under a layer of new sediment. When time has passed and the weight of successive layers has pressed the sediment into sedimentary rock, the hard or bony structure of the buried plant or animal will have left its print there . . . waiting to be unearthed by the fossil-hunter's hammer!

The earth's mountain-building forces may bend and buckle ancient seabeds into mountains, carrying fossils of sea life with them. Fossils of sea animals on lofty peaks used to be thought of as tricks of the Devil, or as

48 evidence of the Bible's Great Flood. Today

The undisputed giants of life were certainly the dinosaurs, or "terrible lizards," that inhabited the earth for some 160 million years, from the Triassic to the Cretaceous periods. Some dinosaurs were vegetarians; but Tyrannosaurus Rex, shown here, was a mighty carnivore. Dinosaurs became extinct inexplicably. It is possible that a change in the world's climate caused their death.

Man to same scale, shown for comparison.

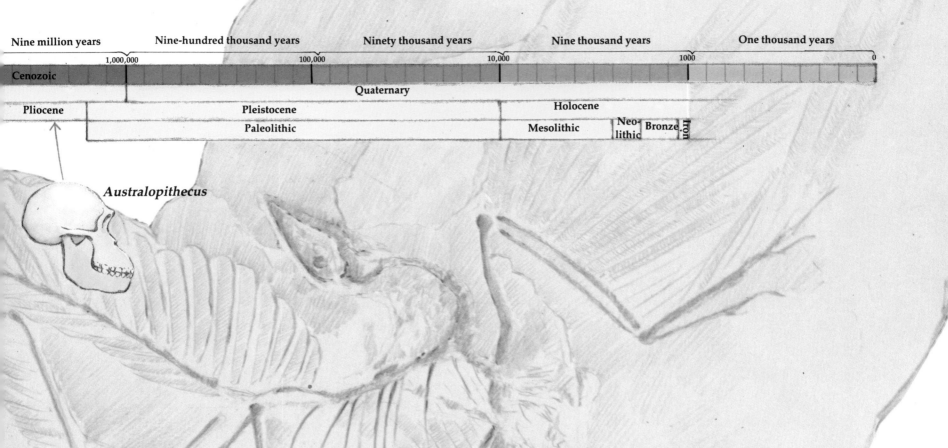

Nine million years	Nine-hundred thousand years	Ninety thousand years	Nine thousand years	One thousand years
	1,000,000	100,000	10,000	1000	0

Cenozoic

Quaternary

Pliocene	Pleistocene		Holocene	
	Paleolithic		Mesolithic	Neo-lithic	Bronze	Iron

Australopithecus

This ancient reptilian bird, Archaernis, was captured in detail by fossilization . . . almost as if in mid-flight!

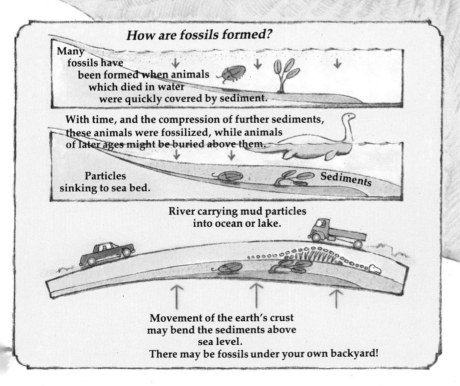

How are fossils formed?

Many fossils have been formed when animals which died in water were quickly covered by sediment.

With time, and the compression of further sediments, these animals were fossilized, while animals of later ages might be buried above them.

Particles sinking to sea bed. — Sediments

River carrying mud particles into ocean or lake.

Movement of the earth's crust may bend the sediments above sea level. There may be fossils under your own backyard!

we see them as visual proof of the perpetual change and movement of the earth's crust.

Naturally, the deeper a sedimentary layer is, the older it is. Fossils found in deep layers are older than those found in recent sediments. Reading the earth's crust from the bottom up, we can follow the evolution of life from primitive plants, through trilobites, dinosaurs, early mammals, right up to our ancestors, the first upright men.

Fossils can be read like nature's photo album, enabling us to relive moments of the earth's past . . . millions of years ago!

49

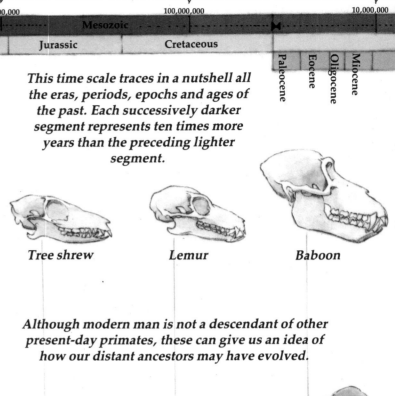

Nine billion years

Nine-hundred million years

Ninety million years

1,000,000,000   100,000,000   10,000,000

Paleozoic   Mesozoic

Triassic | Jurassic | Cretaceous

Pre-Cambrian / Cambrian / Ordovician / Silurian / Devonian / Carboniferous / Permian

Paleocene / Eocene / Oligocene / Miocene

This time scale traces in a nutshell all the eras, periods, epochs and ages of the past. Each successively darker segment represents ten times more years than the preceding lighter segment.

Tree shrew   *Lemur*   *Baboon*

Although modern man is not a descendant of other present-day primates, these can give us an idea of how our distant ancestors may have evolved.

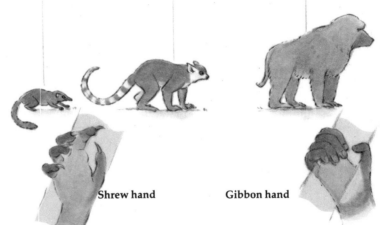

Shrew hand   Gibbon hand

Here is a small dictionary to help you decipher the paleontologists' and anthropologists' difficult terminology. Names are generally derived either from Ancient Greek (Gr), or from Latin (Lat).

. . . To the Uppermost Branches

There is magnificent diversity in the animal world. There are animals of every shape, color and size; flying, swimming or crawling on the earth. Even more fascinating is the order, or similarity, in animals.

All animals are made of cells. They all breathe. Many have similar bone structures. One group of animals within the mammal family has striking similarities with man himself. These animals have man's keen sense of vision, similar bone and skull structures, and fingers and toes capable of grasping and climbing, aided by thumbs. These animals are called primates and include tree-dwelling lemurs, tarsiers, monkeys and apes, as well as man himself.

Charles Darwin's theory of evolution has long been misunderstood by people, for they interpreted it to mean that man is descended from the apes we see in the zoo. This certainly isn't so. The evolution of apes is as long as the evolution of man. But somewhere, far, far back in time, the two species may have had a common ancestor.

Searching for man's ancestors and studying his evolution is called the science of anthropology. Anthropologists learn about ancient man the same way that paleontologists study ancient animals . . . through fossils.

50

-cene, ceno *(Gr)*: new, recent	**Pleisto *(Gr)*: most**
Eo *(Gr)*: early	**Plio *(Gr)*: more**
Holo *(Gr)*: wholly	**-zoic *(Gr)*: life**
-lithic *(Gr)*: stone	**Australo *(Lat)*: southern**
Meso *(Gr)*: middle	**Homo *(Lat)*: man**
Mio *(Gr)*: less	**Erectus *(Lat)*: Upright**
Neo *(Gr)*: new	**Pithecus *(Gr)*: ape**
Oligo *(Gr)*: little	**Sapiens *(Lat)*: wise**
Paleo *(Gr)*: old	**Cro-Magnon:** Name of a cave in France where remains were found.
Neanderthal: A valley in Germany where remains were found.	

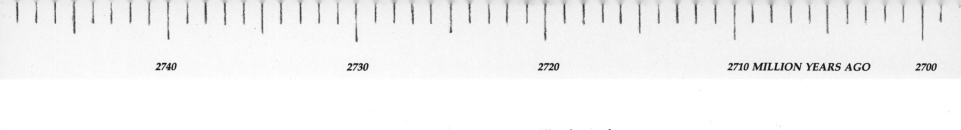

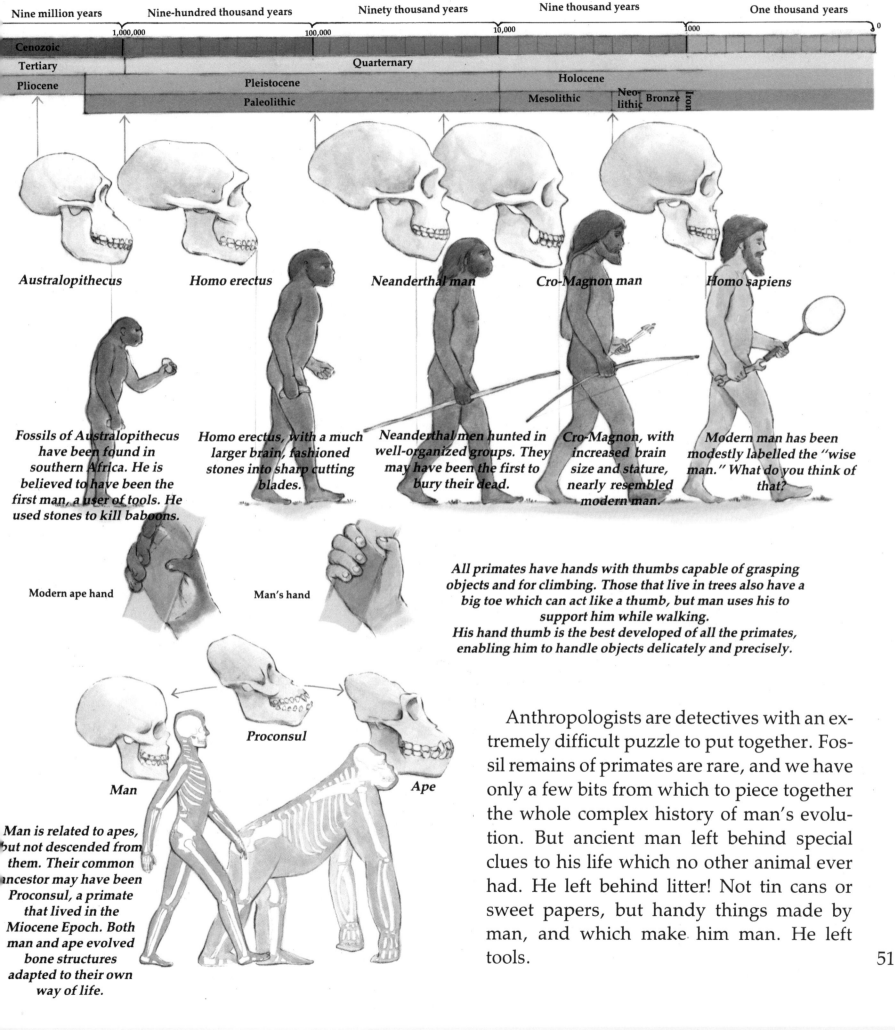

Nine million years	Nine-hundred thousand years	Ninety thousand years	Nine thousand years	One thousand years

1,000,000   100,000   10,000   1000   0

Cenozoic

Tertiary   Quarternary

Pliocene   Pleistocene   Holocene

Paleolithic   Mesolithic   Neo-lithic   Bronze   Iron

Australopithecus   *Homo erectus*   *Neanderthal man*   *Cro-Magnon man*   *Homo sapiens*

Fossils of Australopithecus have been found in southern Africa. He is believed to have been the first man, a user of tools. He used stones to kill baboons.

Homo erectus, with a much larger brain, fashioned stones into sharp cutting blades.

Neanderthal men hunted in well-organized groups. They may have been the first to bury their dead.

Cro-Magnon, with increased brain size and stature, nearly resembled modern man.

Modern man has been modestly labelled the "wise man." What do you think of that?

Modern ape hand   Man's hand

All primates have hands with thumbs capable of grasping objects and for climbing. Those that live in trees also have a big toe which can act like a thumb, but man uses his to support him while walking.
His hand thumb is the best developed of all the primates, enabling him to handle objects delicately and precisely.

Proconsul

Man   *Ape*

Man is related to apes, but not descended from them. Their common ancestor may have been Proconsul, a primate that lived in the Miocene Epoch. Both man and ape evolved bone structures adapted to their own way of life.

Anthropologists are detectives with an extremely difficult puzzle to put together. Fossil remains of primates are rare, and we have only a few bits from which to piece together the whole complex history of man's evolution. But ancient man left behind special clues to his life which no other animal ever had. He left behind litter! Not tin cans or sweet papers, but handy things made by man, and which make him man. He left tools.

51

Man the Maker

For millions of years life existed on earth and no animal made tools. Why did early man? He walked upright and could run, he had good eyesight. But he was nonetheless at a real disadvantage on earth.

First of all, man shared the planet with many other animals who were bigger, stronger and faster than he. Not only did he have to fight for food, he was in constant danger of becoming another animal's dinner!

Secondly, early man had to cope with severe changes in climate. During his evolution our planet several times became very cold. The seas retreated and turned into ice, covering most of the Northern Hemisphere during what we call the Ice Ages. Most plants and animals perished from the cold, but man coped and survived by using his head and his hands. He invented implements and tools which reached farther than his arm, gave strength to his hands, and which were sharper than teeth or claws. With these he fashioned shelter, clothing, and still better tools. We might say that man's inventiveness was triggered by his hungry stomach and his lack of a woolly or furry pelt!

What is remarkable about the first tools man made was that he had no examples to copy. By himself he "saw" in a branch or stick an extension to his arm. He "saw" in a stone a hammer, an axe or a knife. No one was there to show him how to tie a knot, or sew a hide. He found out everything by himself.

Other animals make things too. Beavers build dams, birds make nests, and bees build beehives. There is, however, a distinct dif-

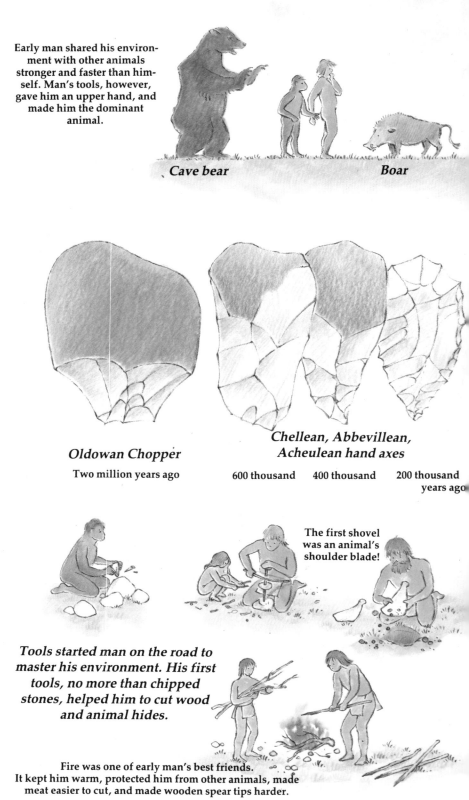

Early man shared his environment with other animals stronger and faster than himself. Man's tools, however, gave him an upper hand, and made him the dominant animal.

Cave bear   *Boar*

Oldowan Chopper

Two million years ago

Chellean, Abbevillean, Acheulean hand axes

600 thousand   400 thousand   200 thousand years ago

The first shovel was an animal's shoulder blade!

Tools started man on the road to master his environment. His first tools, no more than chipped stones, helped him to cut wood and animal hides.

Fire was one of early man's best friends. It kept him warm, protected him from other animals, made meat easier to cut, and made wooden spear tips harder.

ference between what other animals and man make. Other animals build from instinct. Their skills need not be learned. Also, they do not improve them.

Man, on the other hand, from birth must *learn* everything. From his parents, and others, he imitates and is instructed in all he

52

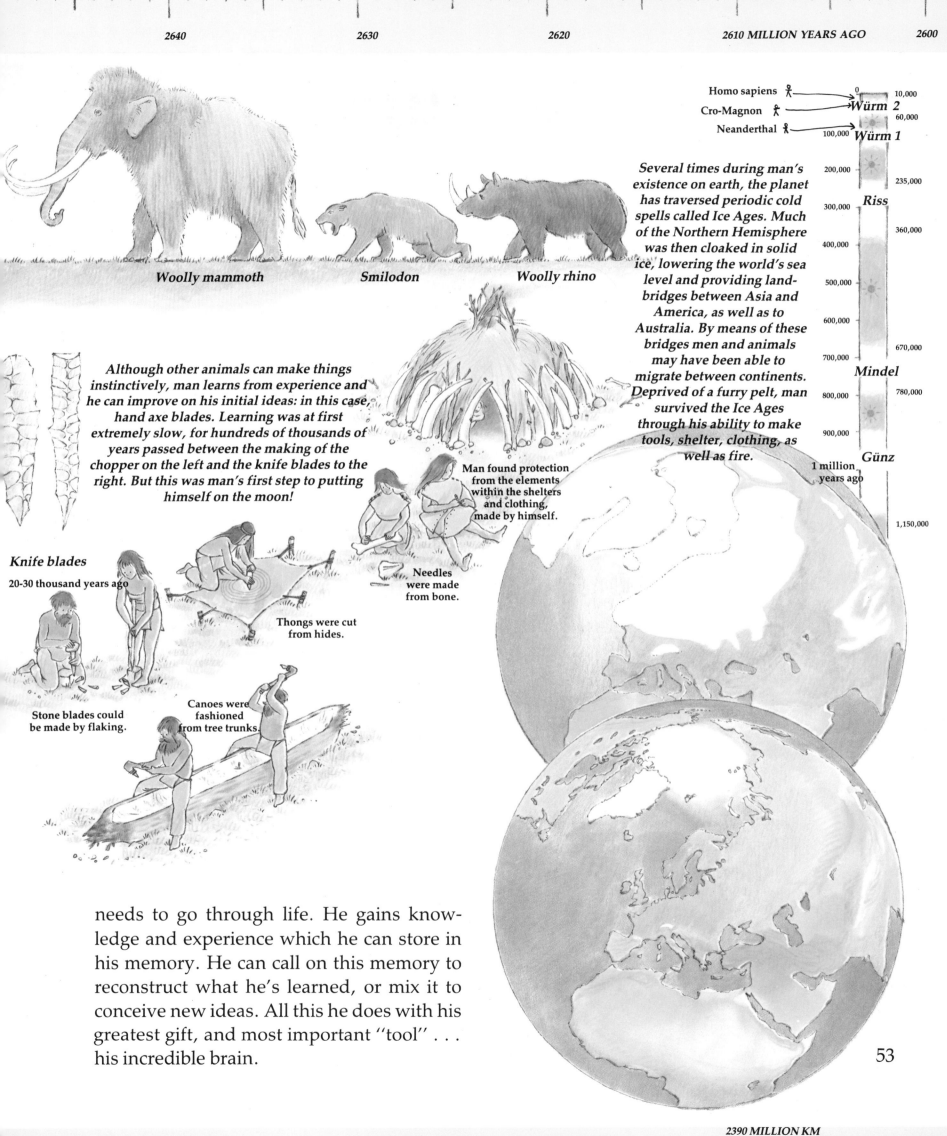

Woolly mammoth

Smilodon

Woolly rhino

Homo sapiens   0
Cro-Magnon   *Würm 2*   10,000
Neanderthal   *Würm 1*   60,000
100,000
200,000   235,000
Riss
300,000   360,000
400,000
500,000
600,000   670,000
Mindel
700,000
800,000   780,000
900,000
1 million years ago   *Günz*
1,150,000

Several times during man's existence on earth, the planet has traversed periodic cold spells called Ice Ages. Much of the Northern Hemisphere was then cloaked in solid ice, lowering the world's sea level and providing land-bridges between Asia and America, as well as to Australia. By means of these bridges men and animals may have been able to migrate between continents. Deprived of a furry pelt, man survived the Ice Ages through his ability to make tools, shelter, clothing, as well as fire.

Although other animals can make things instinctively, man learns from experience and he can improve on his initial ideas: in this case, hand axe blades. Learning was at first extremely slow, for hundreds of thousands of years passed between the making of the chopper on the left and the knife blades to the right. But this was man's first step to putting himself on the moon!

Man found protection from the elements within the shelters and clothing, made by himself.

Knife blades

20-30 thousand years ago

Needles were made from bone.

Thongs were cut from hides.

Stone blades could be made by flaking.

Canoes were fashioned from tree trunks.

needs to go through life. He gains knowledge and experience which he can store in his memory. He can call on this memory to reconstruct what he's learned, or mix it to conceive new ideas. All this he does with his greatest gift, and most important "tool" . . . his incredible brain.

53

Man the Thinker

The brain is certainly one of nature's most incredible creations. Its capability seems to be as limitless as the universe.

The brain's function is to keep the organs of a body working properly and to keep that body alive. At the same time, for humans in particular, it is a "bank" for storing information as memory. Storing knowledge there enables us to learn and to put bits of information together to judge, decide, and get new ideas.

The brain is made up of several distinct parts, and each of these parts has evolved through millions of years to its present size according to its usefulness. Not all animals have brains, only the upper vertebrates, or animals with backbones. The brain of each type of animal has evolved to suit that animal's needs. A fish's brain, for instance, has an extra large portion reserved for eyesight, so the fish can see better underwater. Other animals have an extra-sensitive sense of smell or hearing. The human brain has developed a voluminous bank or warehouse to store all we need to know to go through life! This bank, known as the cerebrum, accounts for around 85 percent of our brain's weight.

What do we mean when we talk about the mind? The brain can be seen as all the different parts put together in our heads, but the mind is more difficult to describe. The mind is basically what the brain *does*. The mind is thought, memory, emotion, action, sensation, perception, and so on. Very little is really known about the mind, it is so complex. For instance, we don't know if the mind is physical matter, or if it is something immaterial and immortal – what is sometimes called the soul.

Knowledge is what the mind has stored as memory. You may think that knowing more makes you smarter, but this is not really true. Knowing more can give you more skills, as speaking many languages lets you talk to many more people. Knowledge is necessary to do a job well, and to make everyday decisions. But knowledge is not truth. Knowing that something is *so*, only means we *believe* it to be so. Saying "I know" means only "I think I know." What you know from the past may not be true in the present, or disproven in the future. Information you read or hear may not be correct in the first place. Understanding the limits of knowledge gives one an open mind.

And so what is intelligence? It used to be thought that the bigger one's brain, the more intelligent one was. This isn't so. Man's brain is big so it can store lots of knowledge. Encyclopedias and computers store lots of knowledge, but neither is intelligent. Intelligence, to put it simply, is "paying attention." An intelligent mind uses knowledge like a reference library, but it needs no books to "see" clearly.

54

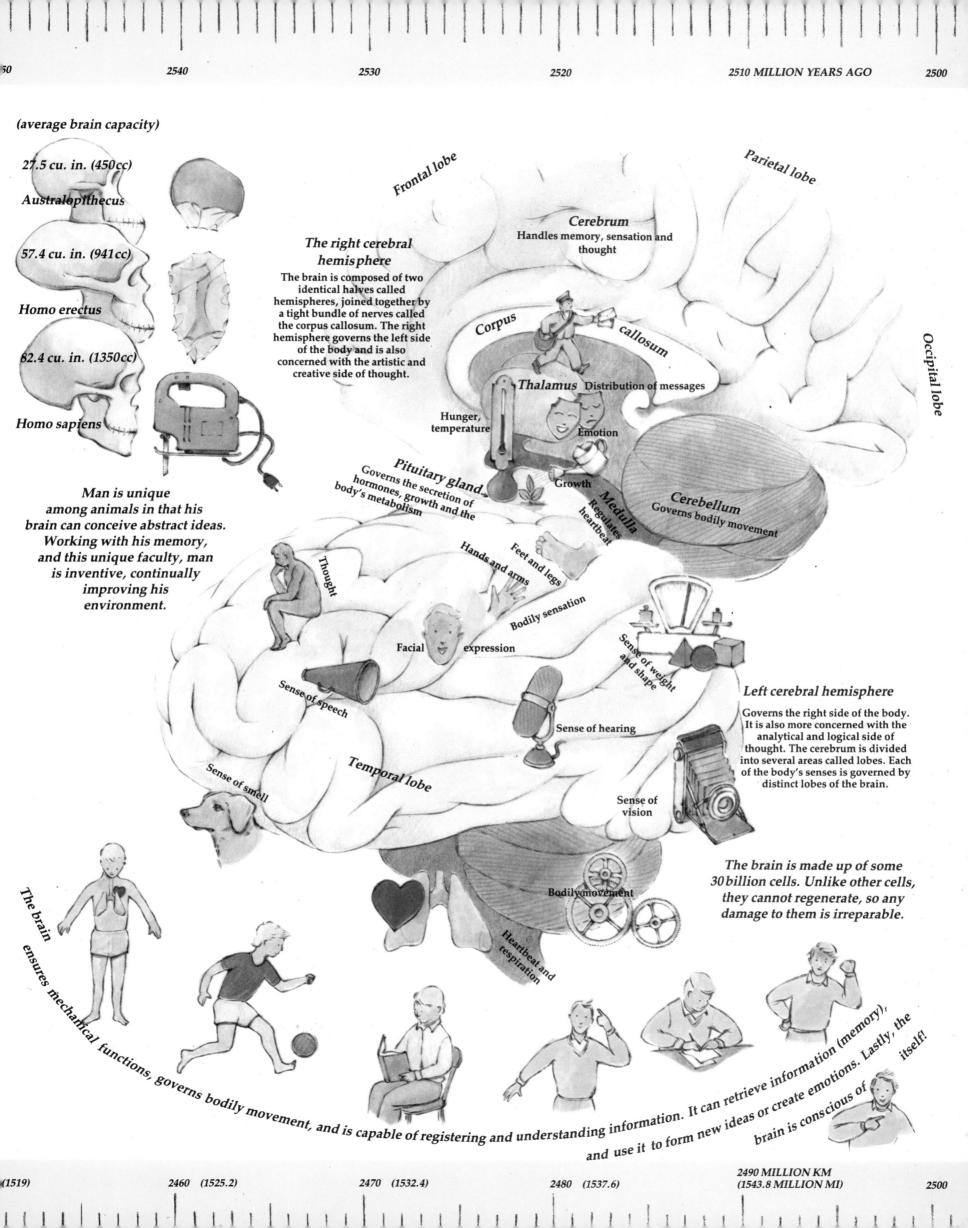

(average brain capacity)

27.5 cu. in. (450cc)

Australopithecus

57.4 cu. in. (941cc)

Homo erectus

82.4 cu. in. (1350cc)

Homo sapiens

Man is unique among animals in that his brain can conceive abstract ideas. Working with his memory, and this unique faculty, man is inventive, continually improving his environment.

The right cerebral hemisphere

The brain is composed of two identical halves called hemispheres, joined together by a tight bundle of nerves called the corpus callosum. The right hemisphere governs the left side of the body and is also concerned with the artistic and creative side of thought.

Frontal lobe

Parietal lobe

Occipital lobe

Cerebrum
Handles memory, sensation and thought

Corpus **callosum**

Thalamus Distribution of messages

Hunger, temperature

Emotion

Pituitary gland
Governs the secretion of hormones, growth and the body's metabolism

Growth

Medulla
Regulates heartbeat

Cerebellum
Governs bodily movement

Thought

Hands and arms

Feet and legs

Bodily sensation

Facial expression

Sense of weight and shape

Sense of speech

Sense of hearing

Left cerebral hemisphere

Governs the right side of the body. It is also more concerned with the analytical and logical side of thought. The cerebrum is divided into several areas called lobes. Each of the body's senses is governed by distinct lobes of the brain.

Sense of smell

Temporal lobe

Sense of vision

The brain is made up of some 30 billion cells. Unlike other cells, they cannot regenerate, so any damage to them is irreparable.

Bodily movement

Heartbeat and respiration

The brain ensures mechanical functions, governs bodily movement, and is capable of registering and understanding information. It can retrieve information (memory), and use it to form new ideas or create emotions. Lastly, the brain is conscious of itself!

Man the Inquirer

Science has provided us with answers to many questions about our physical world, but numerous fields remain barely explored, or seem unattainable. The forces in the universe – those behind atoms, the actions of the mind, and the incredible order throughout all of nature – fill us with awe and wonder.

Prehistoric man had no science, and much less knowledge of the world than we have today. He must have been baffled and frightened by thunderstorms; amazed at the sight of fire, a rare occurrence. He watched the sun and moon travel across the sky, but had no idea why. The death of his parents and comrades would have left him confused.

It was evident to him that some other more powerful forces governed his environment. Was it not natural that man should wish to stay on good terms with these forces, that they might be favorable to him? Perhaps this is where man's spiritual beliefs began; but it is only a guess, for he left little evidence behind him.

Anthropologists have tried to piece together the meaning behind the few relics we have of man's early spiritual life. The most beautiful pieces of evidence are surely the paintings left deep inside caves. These magnificent, stylized pictures of animals were certainly not drawn just for fun, or even to be seen by others. They were painted in the most inaccessible part of a cave,

Early man had no scientific explanations to help him understand the world he lived in. In his wonderment and fear of nature's actions, he was certain of one thing: there was some greater power exerting its force over everything on earth.

An older member of a tribe, respected for his wisdom, may have been thought to have skills in communicating with superhuman powers. This wise man, or shaman, conducted rituals and was called on to take the members of the tribe through the rites of life – just as a priest today performs baptisms, weddings and funerals.

Bear skull burials may have been primitive sacrifices to ensure the continuity of game to hunt. The burial of deceased men, often with their belongings, testify to man's early belief in an afterlife.

56

Here is an orbiting electron of the atom whose

200,000   100,000   50,000   25,000   0   2000

Flake tools   Bear skull   Cave painting   Today

Neanderthal man

Cro-Magnon man
Homo sapiens

New Stone Age →

*Cave painting
of a bison,
Altamira,
Spain*

*Early man was already a master
artist, and caves were
his cathedrals!*

*The Venuses of
Lespugue, France . . .*

. . . and of Willendorf, Austria.

To ensure the continuity of the
tribe, early sculptors may have
made these Venuses to win the
favors of a fertility god.

where not even light would penetrate. You have probably heard of voodoo dolls, into which medicine men stick pins to inflict a wound on whomever the doll represents. Prehistoric man probably believed that his painting had similar powers. By painting an animal, he "controlled" its spirit. He would sometimes draw arrows over the animal, probably to ensure its capture in the next hunt.

Early man also paid tribute to the powers who "made" the animals. He would offer the powers parts of the captured animal, usually the skull and some bones, by burying them carefully. This way he thought that the powers would continue to provide more animals to hunt.

There were no doctors to take care of people who were ill, and presumably many sicknesses were fatal. People didn't live long. To ensure that a tribe did not die out, it was important that mothers had as many children as possible. Early man may have carved the numerous little Venus statuettes which had been believed to ensure fertility and the continuance of his tribe.

The cave paintings and the statuettes are evidence of man's belief in magic. Special rituals were doubtless performed regularly, conducted by an older member of the tribe, called the shaman. The shaman may have communicated with the powers, and guided the tribe with his advice.

57

nucleus is on page 18, 33 ft (10 meters) away!

Man the Speaker

Most animals on earth communicate in one way or another. Blessed with senses to receive information, they have developed various ways of sending information as well.

Communications among animals are known as displays. Displays serve a variety of purposes. As a means of identification, a bird's call can attract a suitable mate. Its song can also warn others of impending danger. Other displays can indicate an animal's intentions.

Each animal has developed its own way of "speaking" to others, suited to its needs. An ant may show another ant where there is food by releasing scent on a trail. A bee, having found flowers with nectar, will do a dance back at the beehive, indicating the route to all the others. Deep at the bottom of the ocean there is no light at all, but some fish live there, equipped with their own lanterns. They are capable of making an electric current which lights them up like a bright neon sign!

"Badging" is communication, too. We can tell a robin by its bright red chest, and a zebra by its stripes. All these communications, however, are little more than signals. Animals cannot relate a story, or express an idea. They lack one thing: language. We humans take language for granted, but have you ever thought how you would live without it? How would you convey your wishes, or ask a question?

Without language, there would be no society, no culture, no arts, or ideas. Have you ever thought what language *is*? We can think in pictures, but mostly we think in language.

Language is a way of thinking. It is also the expression of thought! Language and thought are woven like fabric. One weave supports the other. We do not know how language began. Man had certainly been speaking for hundreds of thousands of years before he began writing.

Languages are alive and change with time and where they are spoken. People of one language may borrow words from another, and drop old words which have become obsolete. Languages have been so mixed together that many languages share common, basic vocabularies: words which stand for the same thing, and which sound alike. Just as brothers and sisters share traits of the same parents, some words share traits of a parent language. Languages with a related basic vocabulary make up a family of languages, probably descended from a parent language.

There are several families of language on earth. One of the biggest is the Indo-European family, whose members include languages from Europe to India. Other families include the Sino-Tibetan, the Altaic, and the African Negro family, to name but a few. There is probably no original language, any more than there was an original man. Nor is any language better than another. Some languages sound musical, others a bit dry, but all languages are above all a means of cooperation between men.

Cooperation means understanding, working together, building together. Thanks to language, that is just what early man began to do.

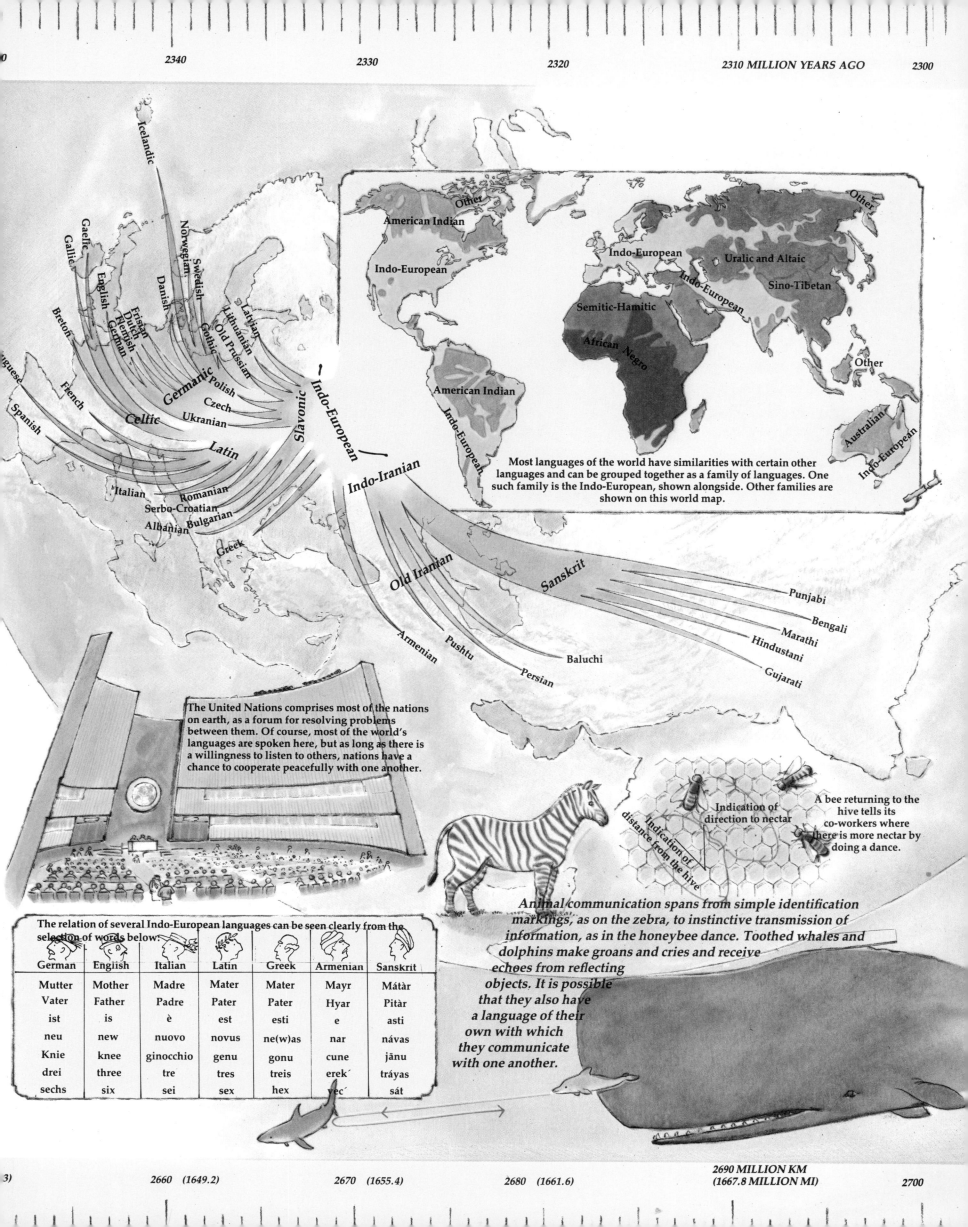

Most languages of the world have similarities with certain other languages and can be grouped together as a family of languages. One such family is the Indo-European, shown alongside. Other families are shown on this world map.

The United Nations comprises most of the nations on earth, as a forum for resolving problems between them. Of course, most of the world's languages are spoken here, but as long as there is a willingness to listen to others, nations have a chance to cooperate peacefully with one another.

A bee returning to the hive tells its co-workers where there is more nectar by doing a dance.

Indication of direction to nectar

Indication of distance from the hive

Animal communication spans from simple identification markings, as on the zebra, to instinctive transmission of information, as in the honeybee dance. Toothed whales and dolphins make groans and cries and receive echoes from reflecting objects. It is possible that they also have a language of their own with which they communicate with one another.

The relation of several Indo-European languages can be seen clearly from the selection of words below:

German	English	Italian	Latin	Greek	Armenian	Sanskrit
Mutter	Mother	Madre	Mater	Mater	Mayr	Mátàr
Vater	Father	Padre	Pater	Pater	Hyar	Pitàr
ist	is	è	est	esti	e	asti
neu	new	nuovo	novus	ne(w)as	nar	návas
Knie	knee	ginocchio	genu	gonu	cune	jânu
drei	three	tre	tres	treis	erek´	tráyas
sechs	six	sei	sex	hex	vec´	sát

From Hunter to Herder

Early man lived as a hunter. He survived the Ice Age thanks to the skill of his hands, the cunning of his brain, and his gift for learning, aided by speech.

Generation after generation, he was always on the move, in the wake of the roaming herds he relied on for food. When the ice which covered much of the Northern Hemisphere retreated, as the earth warmed up, the face of the planet took on a new appearance. The melted ice filled the oceans and made them rise, covering numerous land-bridges which formerly joined the continents. Life on the planet changed too, as animals like the woolly mammoth and reindeer moved north and different, smaller animals came to live in the great forests which grew up from wasteland. Along wide rivers and lakes man not only hunted animals but caught fish, too, with traps, hooks and harpoons.

One day, returning from a hunt, someone may have brought back to camp the babies of

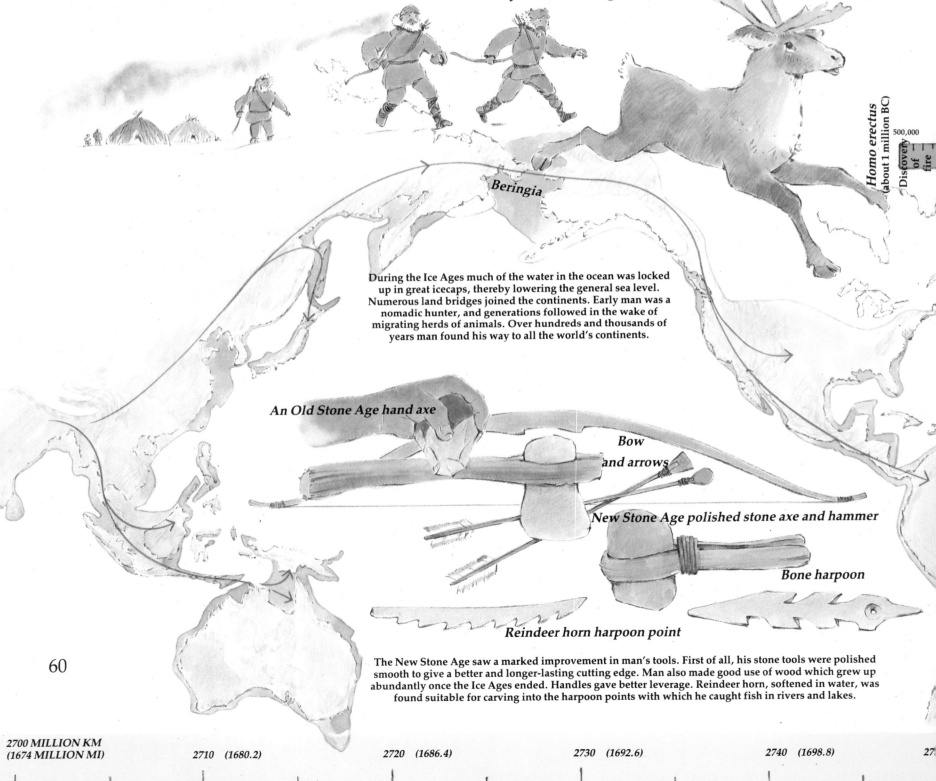

Homo erectus (about 1 million BC)

Discovery of fire 500,000

Beringia

During the Ice Ages much of the water in the ocean was locked up in great icecaps, thereby lowering the general sea level. Numerous land bridges joined the continents. Early man was a nomadic hunter, and generations followed in the wake of migrating herds of animals. Over hundreds and thousands of years man found his way to all the world's continents.

An Old Stone Age hand axe

Bow and arrows

New Stone Age polished stone axe and hammer

Bone harpoon

Reindeer horn harpoon point

The New Stone Age saw a marked improvement in man's tools. First of all, his stone tools were polished smooth to give a better and longer-lasting cutting edge. Man also made good use of wood which grew up abundantly once the Ice Ages ended. Handles gave better leverage. Reindeer horn, softened in water, was found suitable for carving into the harpoon points with which he caught fish in rivers and lakes.

the captured prey. These young animals may have been brought up by the tribe as pets, but it was evident, too, that once fully grown they would also make a good meal! Man had discovered that if he kept animals, he would no longer need to hunt them.

We have no idea when or how man first became domesticated, but it would bring a big change in the way he lived. First of all, he had more food. He tended goats which gave milk, pigs which gave meat, and sheep which also gave wool for clothing. Without the need to hunt, people could live longer in one place, and they built the first settle-

ments, making huts from the materials at hand, be it mud, clay, grass or wood.

With better food and living conditions, people lived longer, and the population grew bigger. Children and old people alike found new tasks, such as tending the herd or gathering berries, fruit and wild grain – from which, it was discovered, bread could be made.

For the first time, man lived "at home." To distinguish this new sedentary life from the old nomadic one, historians have given this age the name Neolithic, or New Stone Age.

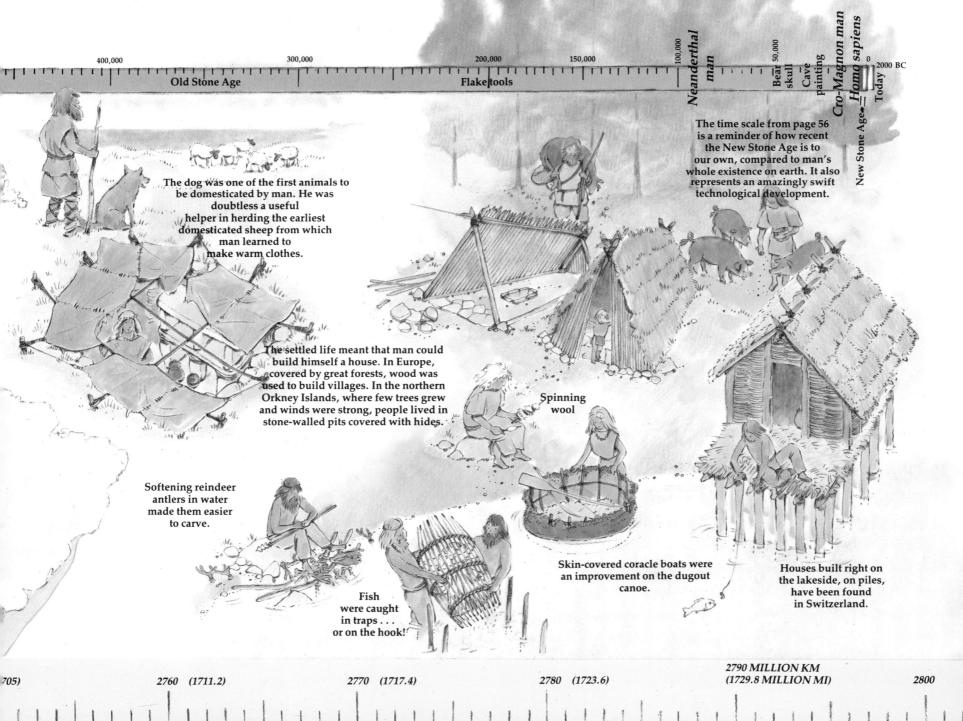

400,000   300,000   200,000   150,000   100,000   50,000   0   2000 BC

Old Stone Age   Flake tools

Neanderthal man   *Bear skull*   *Cave painting*   *Cro-Magnon man*   *Homo sapiens*   *Today*

New Stone Age

The time scale from page 56 is a reminder of how recent the New Stone Age is to our own, compared to man's whole existence on earth. It also represents an amazingly swift technological development.

The dog was one of the first animals to be domesticated by man. He was doubtless a useful helper in herding the earliest domesticated sheep from which man learned to make warm clothes.

The settled life meant that man could build himself a house. In Europe, covered by great forests, wood was used to build villages. In the northern Orkney Islands, where few trees grew and winds were strong, people lived in stone-walled pits covered with hides.

Spinning wool

Softening reindeer antlers in water made them easier to carve.

Fish were caught in traps . . . or on the hook!

Skin-covered coracle boats were an improvement on the dugout canoe.

Houses built right on the lakeside, on piles, have been found in Switzerland.

Of Herders and Harvesters

On page 35, we saw that rivers carry back to the sea the water that once originated there and fell as precipitation. Through the forces of friction and gravity, the rivers also wear away at the earth, eroding it and transporting mud, silt and bits of rocks and minerals downstream. Much of this suspended earth is rich in chemicals that plants need to grow. When this earth piles up on an alluvial plain, where the river meets the sea, it makes a good rich soil for plants to grow in. Similarly, should the river brim over after a season of rains, it will leave on the flooded lands this same enriching earth. It was on the banks of such flooding rivers that man learned the secret of making plants grow.

No one knows just how, when or where farming was started, but the earliest traces of it have been found around five rivers in the Near East and Asia: the Nile, the Tigris, the Euphrates, the Indus, and the Yellow River in China. All these rivers rejuvenated the soil on their river banks with their annual flooding and deposits of silt. There was probably no one place where farming first started. Doubtless, sedentary peoples who had mastered animal domestication had more time to observe their environment and take note of nature's cycles, and perhaps took time to experiment.

62

Farming was the first

People gathered their first harvests where wild grains grew naturally, in the Near East, as early as 7000-8000 years ago. Grain stalks were cut with simple sickles, and the seeds were separated from the shell under a stone-studded sled dragged over the stalks. The nourishing seeds were chewed alone, or mixed with water as porridge, and eventually baked on hot stones as bread.

Mesopotamia

Tigris

Euphrates

Nile Valley

Nile

Present coast

Floodwater laden with silt from upstream

After the flood . . .

. . . silt is left behind on the river banks.

Man began to farm where he had a good chance of sucess: on the fertile river banks left by the rejuvenating floodwaters of certain rivers. Once planted in this fertile ground, seeds had no trouble in growing quickly into tall stalks.

secret man learned from nature, and the golden stalks of grain were his first riches.

Barley

Wild einkorn wheat

Wild emmer wheat

Yellow River Valley

Yellow River

The first cultivated grains were einkorn and emmer wheat, as well as barley, which is especially resistant and adaptable to different climates and grows quickly.

Rice

Rice and millet were the original grains cultivated in China, wheat being introduced from the West around 1300 B.C.

Here are two primitive sickles with which man gleaned the first grains to make his bread. The one above is made with flint edges, while the one below is of clay.

Indus Valley

Indus

When people discovered that a planted seed would yield a new plant, they were able to ''remake'' nature to their own advantage, selecting, breeding and cultivating what was useful . . . and eliminating what was not.

The domestication of animals, and of the land, gave man all he needed to satisfy his stomach! It also gave him the time and inspiration to improve his environment in every way. His inventive mind was set to work!

63

Something Borrowed, Something New

Ever since Old Stone Age man made his first simple tools he has been constantly improving them. The inventions made today may be more complex, but the incentive and mental action behind them have been the same for thousands of years: the need to make things better, to do jobs more easily.

Most inventions have been made by borrowing from other things which already exist. Early man's flint-cutting blade was made easier to use by adding a handle. By varying the shape of both blade and handle, man made a variety of specialized and properly adapted tools. Other inventions, however, may be entirely new.

Each new invention eased the job to be done, and each gave man a little more mastery over his environment. On the other

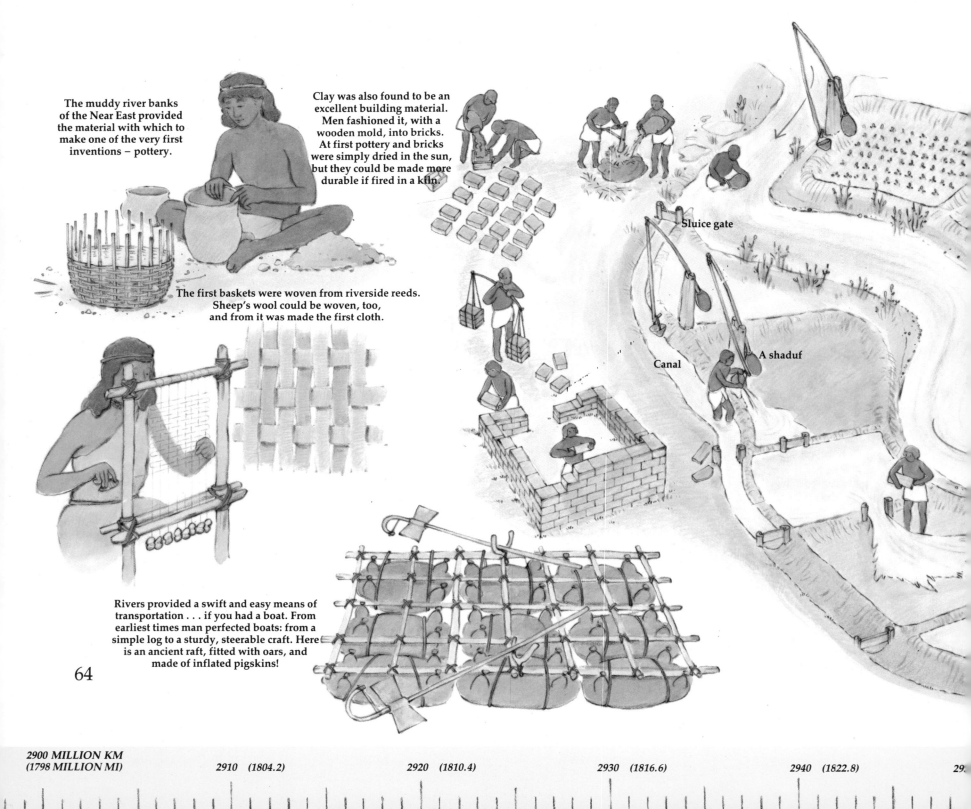

The muddy river banks of the Near East provided the material with which to make one of the very first inventions – pottery.

Clay was also found to be an excellent building material. Men fashioned it, with a wooden mold, into bricks. At first pottery and bricks were simply dried in the sun, but they could be made more durable if fired in a kiln.

Sluice gate

The first baskets were woven from riverside reeds. Sheep's wool could be woven, too, and from it was made the first cloth.

Canal

A shaduf

Rivers provided a swift and easy means of transportation . . . if you had a boat. From earliest times man perfected boats: from a simple log to a sturdy, steerable craft. Here is an ancient raft, fitted with oars, and made of inflated pigskins!

64

hand most inventions, while solving one problem, created another! This is why invention has never ceased. Invention creates the need to invent!

When man travelled on his first boat, a drifting log, he needed to invent an oar to propel and steer it. This worked fine on a pond or river, but at sea he needed a sail.

A good house could be built from mud bricks, but many houses built together required notions of engineering, measuring and drainage.

Man enlarged his farmland with irrigation systems, but this required expert organization and measurement of time. He would have needed numbers and a means of recording them: the invention was called writing!

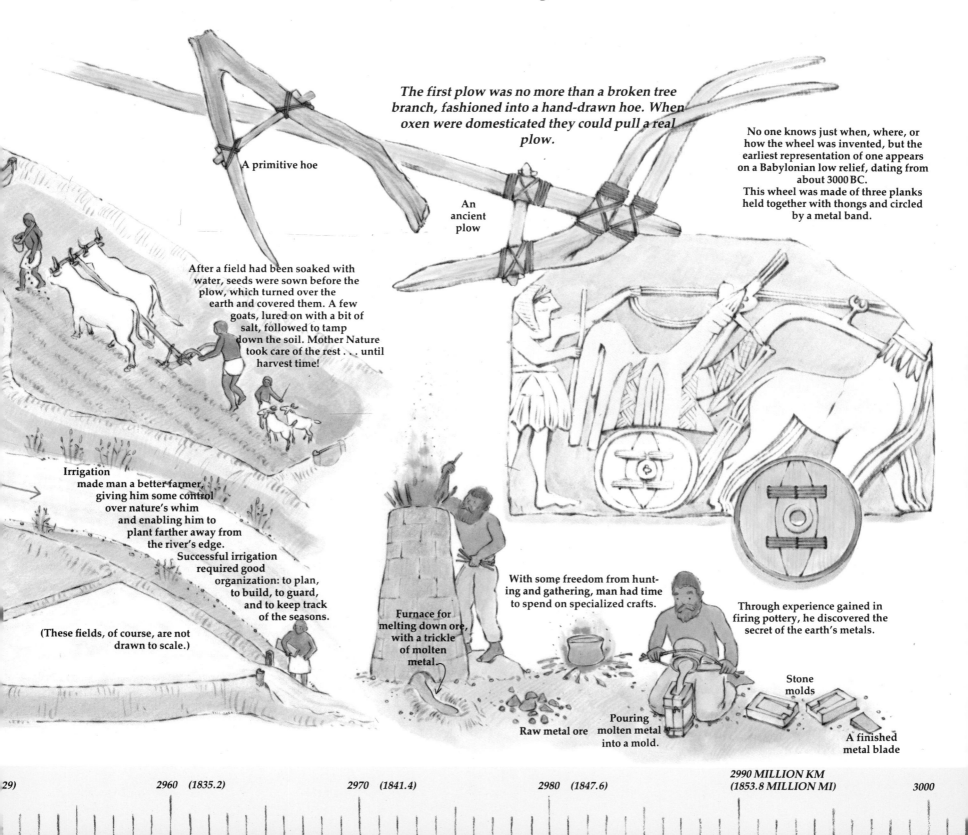

A primitive hoe

The first plow was no more than a broken tree branch, fashioned into a hand-drawn hoe. When oxen were domesticated they could pull a real plow.

An ancient plow

No one knows just when, where, or how the wheel was invented, but the earliest representation of one appears on a Babylonian low relief, dating from about 3000 BC.
This wheel was made of three planks held together with thongs and circled by a metal band.

After a field had been soaked with water, seeds were sown before the plow, which turned over the earth and covered them. A few goats, lured on with a bit of salt, followed to tamp down the soil. Mother Nature took care of the rest . . . until harvest time!

Irrigation made man a better farmer, giving him some control over nature's whim and enabling him to plant farther away from the river's edge.
Successful irrigation required good organization: to plan, to build, to guard, and to keep track of the seasons.

(These fields, of course, are not drawn to scale.)

Furnace for melting down ore, with a trickle of molten metal.

With some freedom from hunting and gathering, man had time to spend on specialized crafts.

Through experience gained in firing pottery, he discovered the secret of the earth's metals.

Stone molds

Raw metal ore

Pouring molten metal into a mold.

A finished metal blade

Reading, Writing and 'Rithmetic

Before he could write, man told stories with pictures.

This New Stone Age picture tells us vividly of a hunter's adventure, chased by his prey!

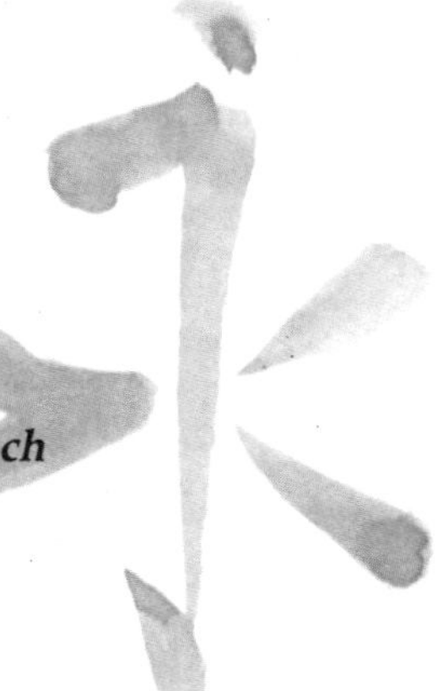

The Chinese written language uses a great number of separate symbols, each of which represent whole words or ideas. This one, which stands for eternity, is but one of some 40,000!

This Babylonian clay tablet is one of the oldest records of writing, dating from about 4000 BC. It was probably a record of accounts.

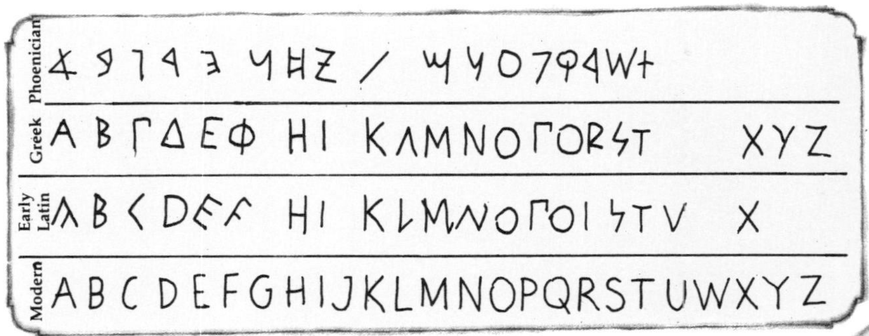

	Phoenician	Æ � ...							

Greek Phoenician: ≮ 𝟗 𝟙 𝟜 𝟛   ⴘⵁⵣ /   ⵤⵤO𝟟𝟗ⵤW𝟙

Greek: A B Γ Δ E Φ   H I   K Λ M N O Γ O P Ϟ T   X Y Z

Early Latin: ∧ B < D E Ϝ   H I   K L M N O Γ O I Ϟ T V   X

Modern: A B C D E F G H I J K L M N O P Q R S T U W X Y Z

Our modern alphabet is the result of a continual development of symbols standing for single, separate sounds. Our word alphabet comes from the names of the first two Greek letters: alpha and beta.

Primitive	Baby-lonian	Egyptian	Roman	Arabic	European	Computer binary	Chinese
I	ⵟo）	I	I	I	1	1	一
II	ⵚⵚ	II	II	ノ	2	10	二
III	ⵚⵚⵚ	III	III	ﬡ	3	11	三
IIII		IIII	IV	ξ	4	100	四
IIIII		IIIII	V	o	5	101	五
		IIIIII	VI	ⴘ	6	110	六
		IIIIIII	VII	∨	7	111	七
		IIIIIIII	VIII	∧	8	1000	八
		IIIIIIIII	IX	ⴳ	9	1001	九
⟨o⦿		∩	X	⼁·	10	1010	十
		ⵍⵍⵍⵍ	L		50		五+
		℮	C		100	1100100	百
		ⴔ	M		1000		千

Counting is doubtless as old as writing. It developed just like writing, finding separate symbols for different quantities, along with the ingenious "place-value" system.

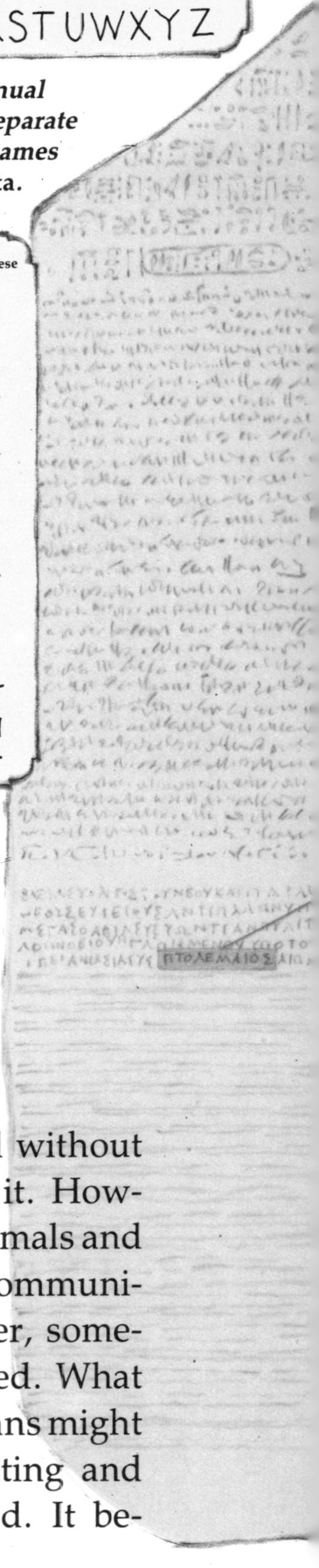

Writing is the one invention which made history . . .

Have you ever imagined how it would be not knowing how to read or write? If you have ever travelled to Greece, Russia, or the Near or Far East, and tried to read the road signs, you'll know just how important written language is. If you can't decipher it, you're lost! We learn how to read and write so soon in life that it seems as natural as speech, but for thousands of years people lived without reading or writing a word. How did they manage?

In prehistoric times people lived without writing because they didn't need it. However, when they learned to tend animals and began to farm, to build their first communities and cooperate with one another, something more than speech was needed. What people heard, they might forget; plans might be misunderstood; dates for planting and reaping might not be remembered. It be-

66

The written symbols on these clay tablets
from the ancient Indus Valley
civilization have not yet been deciphered.

Today, as many people with
different languages to
understand notice quickly,
there has been a return to the use
of simple pictograms.

(Hieroglyphs are read from right to left.)

PTOL M E S
PTOLEMAIOS

ΠΤΟΛΕΜΑΙΟΣ

For centuries the hieroglyphs of the Ancient
Egyptians were a complete mystery. In 1801
a Napoleonic expedition unearthed a dark,
basalt stone engraved in three languages:
hieroglyphs, demotic (Ancient Egyptian
script), and Ancient Greek. Called the
Rosetta Stone, it was a trilingual dictionary
which enabled the Frenchman Jean-François
Champollion (1790–1832) to decode the
Egyptian text. He discovered that the circled
cartouches stood for the name of the then
Pharaoh Ptolemy, and went on from there.
Ancient Egypt, until Champollion's
discovery, was literally a prehistoric age. It
suddenly became one of the best-recorded
periods of ancient history!

. . . for there is no history without writing!

In 1972 the United States sent a space probe, Pioneer 10, into
the universe. Upon it is the plaque below, destined to tell any
extraterrestrial people who might come upon it from where it
has come.

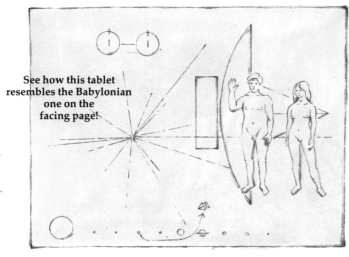

See how this tablet
resembles the Babylonian
one on the
facing page!

came vital to write things down, so that
everybody understood.

Writing did not come about in just one
place only, but in different places at different
times, as people began to need it. Nor was
writing really invented. It evolved over
thousands of years. Even the Ancient Egyptians lived with just the rudiments of writing – they didn't even have a real alphabet!

The simple scratches in clay and stone,

and scribblings with a pen, offered possibili-
ties no other tool possessed. They carried a
person's words farther than the loudest can-
non, and stayed alive long after his own
death. Written accounts made trading much
easier, and a ruler's voice could be heard
over all his land. Indeed, writing was present in everything that man built, believed,
created and planned. It was the cornerstone,
the key, to civilization.

67

Enter Civilization!

Civilization is the largest stage in man's development. It appeared about five to six thousand years ago, and we live in it today. Our present civilization travels faster, communicates better and knows more than any civilization of the past, yet it is basically not very different from those that grew up around the original "cradlelands."

In spite of all the technology man has created, and all the science and history he has learned since the dawn of civilization, man has not changed. Knowledge may have changed our *way of life*, but it has not advanced *life* at all.

It is quite possible, of course, that man has not yet reached a final development, and our descendants of the year 4000 may write of our present age as "the last years of the New Stone Age"!

What does civilization mean? The word comes from the Latin word *civis*, meaning "citizen," the inhabitant of a city. Civilization, it would seem, is culture based around cities. But for the key to understanding what civilization *is*, and how it may have come about, we need to ask further: "What is a city?"

Probably you picture a place with big buildings and noisy traffic. But before that, what is it that all cities, towns, and villages have in common? They are places where people live together and work together, at a *variety of jobs*. Each citizen is a specialist in some kind of work.

Let us look back at New Stone Age man. What happened when he began to farm? First, man changed from a hunter and gatherer of food to a producer of food. As the population began to grow, being better fed, better sheltered, and better clothed, there

68

were more mouths to feed, and man enlarged his arable land by means of irrigation. This early invention challenged him to plan and organize for the first time. Land had to be measured, workers delegated to dig

The Mesopotamian civilizations are characterized by their versatile use of clay. These people imprinted seals on clay, and also inscribed notes on clay tablets held within clay envelopes!

Mesopotamian cuneiform writing is one of the first testimonies to civilization.

The Babylonian King Hammurabi set out one of the earliest codes of public laws on a stone pillar around 1792–1750 BC. Law defines a common standard of behavior for members of a civilization.

This delicately decorated pot comes from the island of Crete and dates from about 1500 BC.

The Egyptian civilization showed a marked preoccupation with life after death, as illustrated by the lavish mummy on the left, as well as the great pyramids.

Nineveh

Mesopotamia

Tigris

Euphrates

(Baghdad)
Babylon
Susa

Uruak

Ur

Alexandria

Giza   Cairo
   Memphis

Nile valley

Thebes

Karnak

Luxor

1st cataract   Aswan

Papyrus

Egyptian scribes kept accounts of daily Egyptian life. They used palettes and brushes like the one here to write on paper made from the stalks of the papyrus plant.

Nile   Abu Simbel

The Egyptians had fine sailing ships with which they traded up and down the Nile River, as well as making expeditions down the unexplored coast of Africa.

The river valleys where the first towns grew up are known as

learn

ditches and food to be distributed to them. Seasons had to be carefully watched to know just when to plant and harvest.

So it happened that not everyone was a farmer. There were engineers, laborers, administrators, scribes and sky-watchers. The community's work was divided into a variety of jobs. Each person became a specialist in his field . . . and so man had civilization!

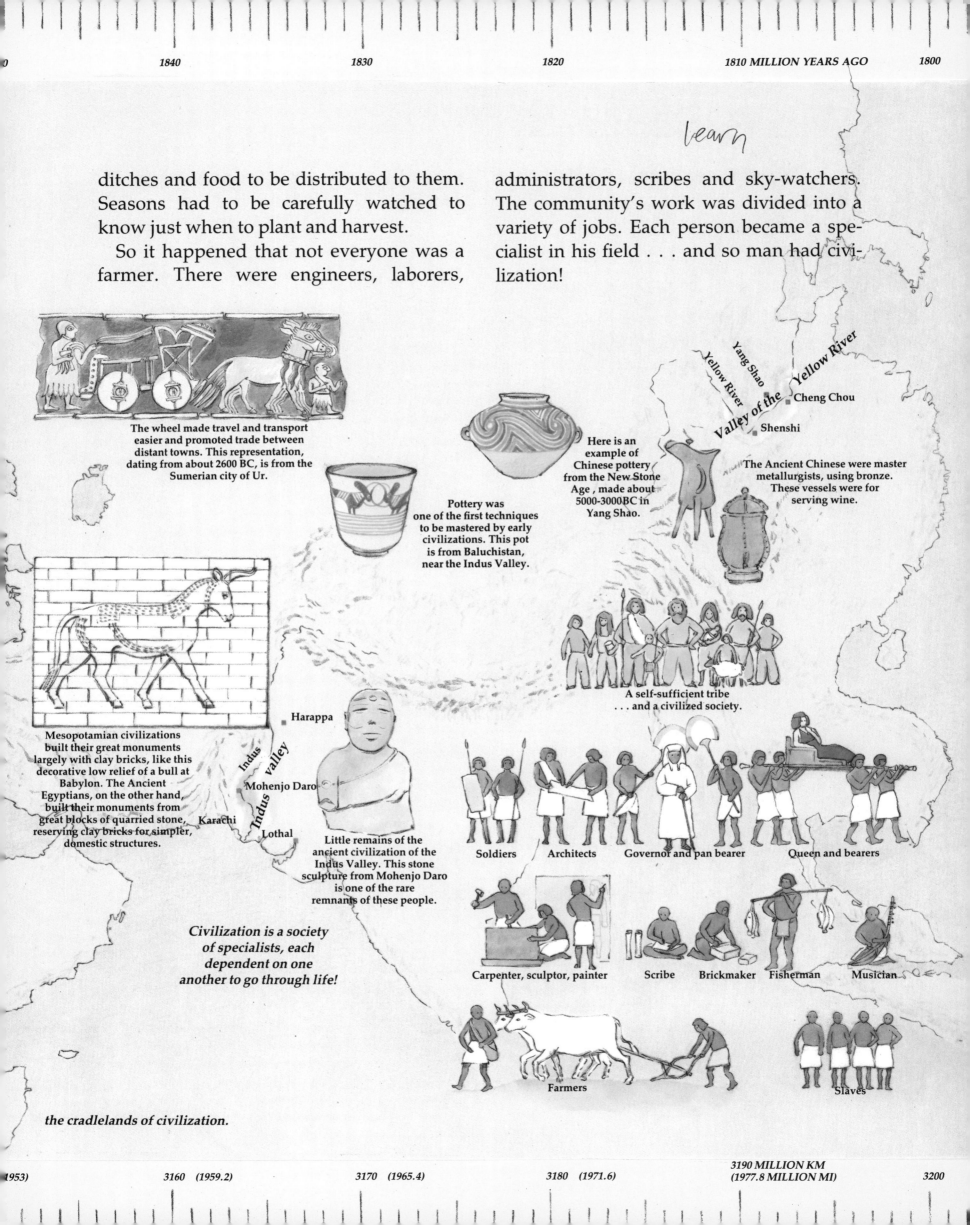

The wheel made travel and transport easier and promoted trade between distant towns. This representation, dating from about 2600 BC, is from the Sumerian city of Ur.

Pottery was one of the first techniques to be mastered by early civilizations. This pot is from Baluchistan, near the Indus Valley.

Here is an example of Chinese pottery from the New Stone Age , made about 5000-3000BC in Yang Shao.

The Ancient Chinese were master metallurgists, using bronze. These vessels were for serving wine.

Yang Shao
Yellow River
Valley of the Yellow River
Cheng Chou
Shenshi

A self-sufficient tribe . . . and a civilized society.

Mesopotamian civilizations built their great monuments largely with clay bricks, like this decorative low relief of a bull at Babylon. The Ancient Egyptians, on the other hand, built their monuments from great blocks of quarried stone, reserving clay bricks for simpler, domestic structures.

Harappa
Indus valley
Mohenjo Daro
Karachi
Lothal
Indus valley

Little remains of the ancient civilization of the Indus Valley. This stone sculpture from Mohenjo Daro is one of the rare remnants of these people.

Civilization is a society of specialists, each dependent on one another to go through life!

Soldiers   Architects   Governor and pan bearer   Queen and bearers

Carpenter, sculptor, painter   Scribe   Brickmaker   Fisherman   Musician

Farmers   Slaves

the cradlelands of civilization.

Of Business and Bondage

People living in civilization are dependent on one another. Each person provides a particular product or service for the others, and receives other products and services in return. Farming provided the first surpluses of food that gave man the time to work at other tasks. One of the earliest industries, metalworking, a difficult and time-consuming activity, became possible only when farmers could produce enough to support people to work metal.

Metalworkers and farmers might barter their products . . . so many tools for so much grain, for instance. However, civilization became more complex and trades more specialized. It was necessary to find some common means of exchange. So money was invented.

What is money? Above all, money is a convenience. Have you ever tried to buy something without it? Imagine you need some new buttons, but only have apples to buy them with. You would have to find someone with extra buttons, who would like to have some apples! Of course, trade like this is impossible, and money solves the problem. Money separates the act of buying from that of selling. You can buy buttons, and the button-man can buy what he wants, when he wants. He accepts your money because he knows other people will easily accept it, too. Thus, money has value because everyone agrees that it does.

Anything rare enough and acceptable to all can be used as money. Indians traded with beads; schoolchildren with marbles; and even cigarettes could buy you what you wanted during the last world war when they were rare and desirable. But from earliest times metal was found to be the most

practical money. It could be divided into small bits, was easily carried, and could be put to a variety of uses as well: to make tools, weapons, containers or jewelry.

When jobs became specialized, with each person skilled at one task, a community's productivity could increase. It could sell what it made in excess to other communities and become wealthier. The more hands that were put to work, the faster and better production became. Labor had to be as cheap as possible, and free at best. Man had learned to harness beasts of burden; surely he could harness his own kind, as slaves?

Societies condoned slavery when they could produce enough food to feed the extra mouths, and needed extra manpower to build up their civilization. A slave was someone owned as the personal property of another, deprived of any rights and obliged to work involuntarily, for free. The earliest slaves were probably the conquered subjects of a rival community; but convicted criminals, and people who had run up unpayable debts could also be made slaves. A debtor might even sell his wife and children as slaves!

Slavery provided much of the manpower that built the cities of Mesopotamia and the temples and pyramids of Egypt. Slaves worked the galleys of the Greek and Roman navies. Reaching a peak in Roman times, slavery persisted for centuries afterwards. The medieval peasant, or serf, had little more rights than an ancient slave.

Only in the last centuries have efforts been made to abolish slavery. But it still persists today in forced labor camps in many countries of the world.

70

Barter Exchange

An apple   for a button.

Monetary Exchange

Money   for a pen . . .   for a button . . .   for an apple.

Money separates the acts of buying and selling. As such, it is a promise of payment. The man who buys a pen with money promises the pen vendor that he will be able to use the same money to buy buttons, apples or anything else! Money is a convenient means of exchange.

Coin representing Alexander the Great

Ancient Athenian coin

Ancient Roman coin depicting Caesar

Money does not make the world go round, but it almost does! Money provides the opportunity for each person to do a different job. It allows the division of labor which is the backbone of civilization.

Roof tiles made by potters

Seafaring merchant

House made by carpenters and masons

Delivery men

Shopkeeper

Soldiers

Market traders

Baker

Entertainer

Road made by engineers

Slave dealer

Fishermen

Water bearer

Peddler

Hunter

Litter bearers

Overseer

Keeping Time with the Sky

On page 28, we saw how the earth's tilt, its rotation, its orbit around the sun and the orbit of its moon make a giant celestial clock which tells us night from day, and the season of the year. Long before mechanical clocks man "told time" by the sky.

Time is told by recurring cycles. A simple cycle to follow is that of day and night, and day again. We can keep track of groups of days by means of a calendar, but before the use of writing people counted groups of days by following the cycle of the moon.

When man became civilized and began to farm by the banks of rivers it was necessary to keep track of a longer cycle which told him the seasons to sow and to reap, and warned

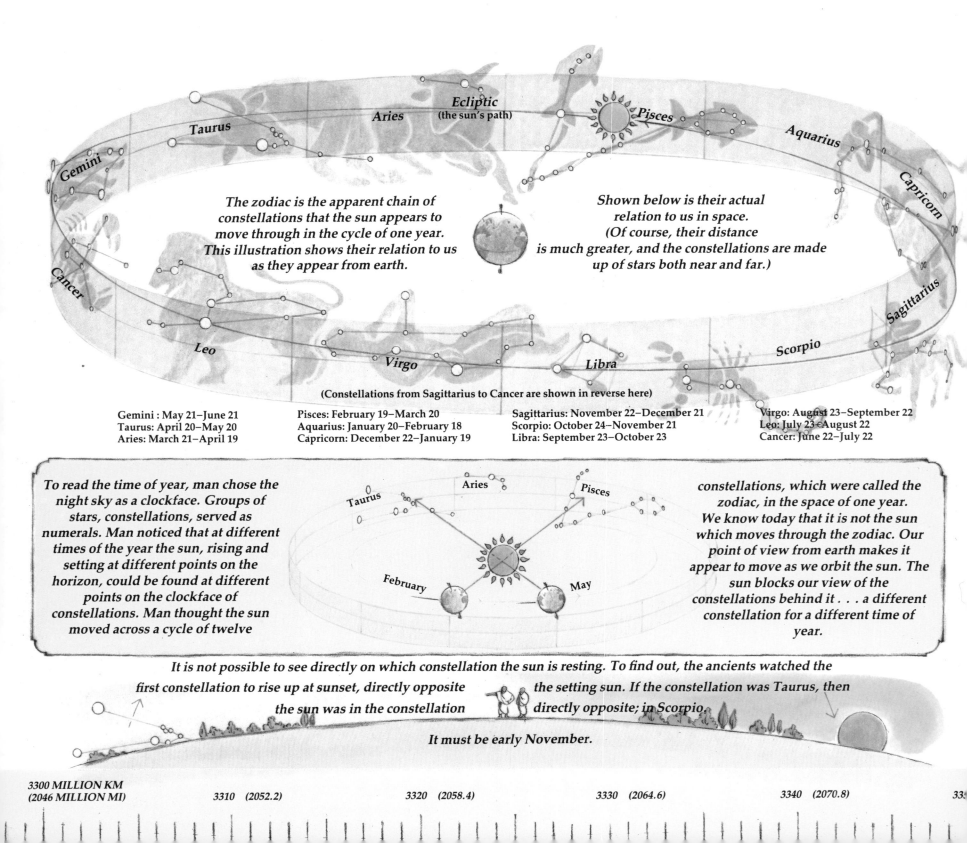

The zodiac is the apparent chain of constellations that the sun appears to move through in the cycle of one year. This illustration shows their relation to us as they appear from earth.

Shown below is their actual relation to us in space. (Of course, their distance is much greater, and the constellations are made up of stars both near and far.)

(Constellations from Sagittarius to Cancer are shown in reverse here)

Gemini : May 21–June 21
Taurus: April 20–May 20
Aries: March 21–April 19

Pisces: February 19–March 20
Aquarius: January 20–February 18
Capricorn: December 22–January 19

Sagittarius: November 22–December 21
Scorpio: October 24–November 21
Libra: September 23–October 23

Virgo: August 23–September 22
Leo: July 23–August 22
Cancer: June 22–July 22

To read the time of year, man chose the night sky as a clockface. Groups of stars, constellations, served as numerals. Man noticed that at different times of the year the sun, rising and setting at different points on the horizon, could be found at different points on the clockface of constellations. Man thought the sun moved across a cycle of twelve constellations, which were called the zodiac, in the space of one year. We know today that it is not the sun which moves through the zodiac. Our point of view from earth makes it appear to move as we orbit the sun. The sun blocks our view of the constellations behind it . . . a different constellation for a different time of year.

It is not possible to see directly on which constellation the sun is resting. To find out, the ancients watched the first constellation to rise up at sunset, directly opposite the setting sun. If the constellation was Taurus, then directly opposite; in Scorpio, the sun was in the constellation

It must be early November.

when the river would flood: a cycle called the year.

The cycle of the year (365¼ days) does not divide into a full number of lunar cycles (29½ days). To make a proper calendar, you have to make some months longer than the moon cycle. Julius Caesar is credited with having established the first practical calendar, and we still use it today (modified by Pope Gregory in 1582), it works so well.

A modern attempt at a world calendar with more regular months has been proposed. This calendar has the advantage that each day of the year, and hence all holidays, fall at the same place every year. That, it seems, is what people want to know today!

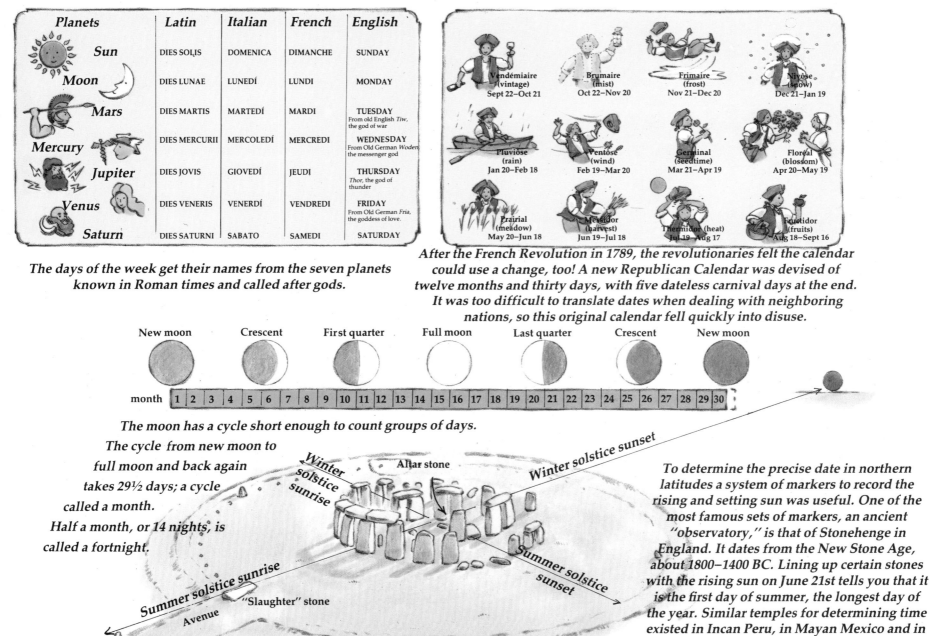

Planets		Latin	Italian	French	English
Sun		DIES SOLIS	DOMENICA	DIMANCHE	SUNDAY
Moon		DIES LUNAE	LUNEDÍ	LUNDI	MONDAY
Mars		DIES MARTIS	MARTEDÍ	MARDI	TUESDAY *From old English Tiw, the god of war*
Mercury		DIES MERCURII	MERCOLEDÍ	MERCREDI	WEDNESDAY *From Old German Woden the messenger god*
Jupiter		DIES JOVIS	GIOVEDÍ	JEUDI	THURSDAY *Thor, the god of thunder*
Venus		DIES VENERIS	VENERDÍ	VENDREDI	FRIDAY *From Old German Fria, the goddess of love.*
Saturn		DIES SATURNI	SABATO	SAMEDI	SATURDAY

The days of the week get their names from the seven planets known in Roman times and called after gods.

Vendémiaire (vintage) Sept 22–Oct 21 · Brumaire (mist) Oct 22–Nov 20 · Frimaire (frost) Nov 21–Dec 20 · Nivôse (snow) Dec 21–Jan 19 · Pluviôse (rain) Jan 20–Feb 18 · Ventôse (wind) Feb 19–Mar 20 · Germinal (seedtime) Mar 21–Apr 19 · Floréal (blossom) Apr 20–May 19 · Prairial (meadow) May 20–Jun 18 · Messidor (harvest) Jun 19–Jul 18 · Thermidor (heat) Jul 19–Aug 17 · Fructidor (fruits) Aug 18–Sept 16

After the French Revolution in 1789, the revolutionaries felt the calendar could use a change, too! A new Republican Calendar was devised of twelve months and thirty days, with five dateless carnival days at the end. It was too difficult to translate dates when dealing with neighboring nations, so this original calendar fell quickly into disuse.

New moon · Crescent · First quarter · Full moon · Last quarter · Crescent · New moon

month | 1 2 3 4 5 6 7 8 9 10 11 12 13 14 15 16 17 18 19 20 21 22 23 24 25 26 27 28 29 30

The moon has a cycle short enough to count groups of days.

The cycle from new moon to full moon and back again takes 29½ days; a cycle called a month. Half a month, or 14 nights, is called a fortnight.

Winter solstice sunrise · Altar stone · Winter solstice sunset · Summer solstice sunrise · Summer solstice sunset · Avenue · "Slaughter" stone · "Heel" stone

To determine the precise date in northern latitudes a system of markers to record the rising and setting sun was useful. One of the most famous sets of markers, an ancient "observatory," is that of Stonehenge in England. It dates from the New Stone Age, about 1800–1400 BC. Lining up certain stones with the rising sun on June 21st tells you that it is the first day of summer, the longest day of the year. Similar temples for determining time existed in Incan Peru, in Mayan Mexico and in Ancient Egypt.

Brilliance from Dark Ages

Here are some waterwheel types

Overshot

Breastshot

Undershot, or stream

The Roman chariot horses above strangle themselves the harder they pull. The shoulder harness, below, puts the pressure in the proper place.

Shoulder harness

Moldboard

With sturdier plows and more powerful horses, and thanks to proper harnessing, farming tasks were speeded up.

Fallow (or unsown field)

Wheat or rye

Barley or beans

Medieval farmers practiced crop rotation, which allowed the soil to rest and rejuvenate after providing a year's harvest.

The first windmills appeared in Europe in the 1100s, probably adapted from windmills in central Asia. Vertical watermills were first built on the Tiber, in Rome, in AD 536. The elaborate gearing used gave men the idea for making the first clocks.

Horseshoes gave hooves a better hold on the ground.

The energy needed to build the great, ancient civilizations of the Mediterranean came from manpower: the muscles of the abundant slaves who carried out every varied task necessary to till the land, man the ships and build the cities. Although they were skilled engineers, superb artists and able administrators, the ancient civilizations of Egypt, Greece, and Rome added few technological innovations.

The period following the fall of the Roman Empire, the last of the great, ancient civilizations, is sometimes called the Dark Ages. Often thought of as a sombre age of stagnant minds, barbaric invasions and poverty, these times nonetheless witnessed the birth of a whole host of inventions to ease work and quicken travel.

New plows with iron blades and moldboards were made, strong enough to turn the wet and heavy soil of northern Europe. Horses were stronger and worked faster than the slow Mediterranean oxen, thanks to proper harnesses and sturdy iron

74

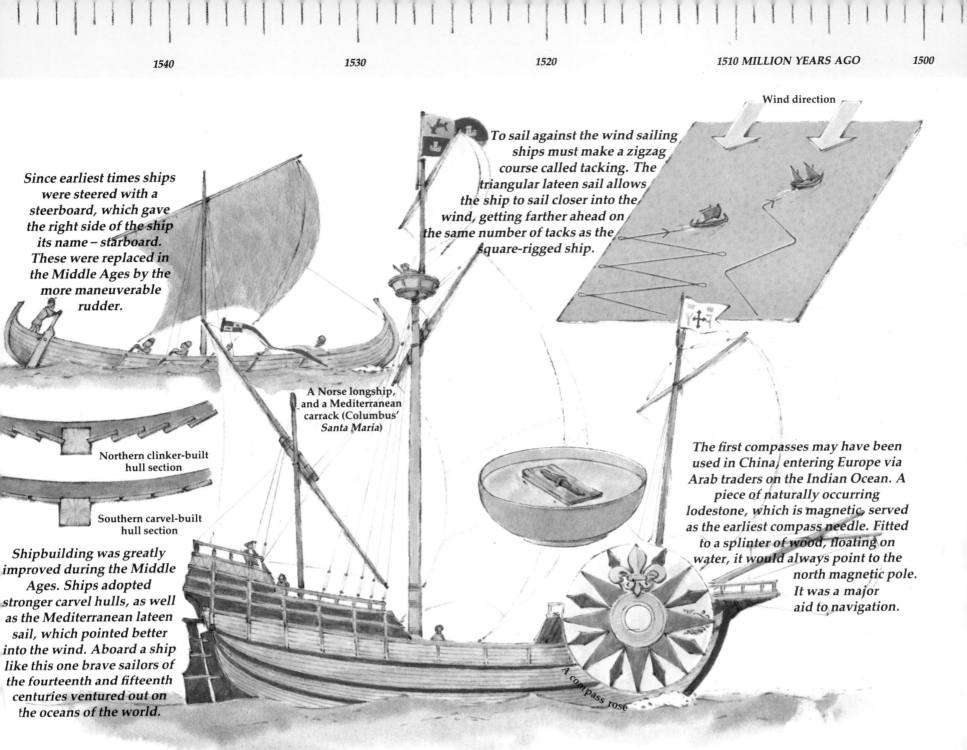

Since earliest times ships were steered with a steerboard, which gave the right side of the ship its name – starboard. These were replaced in the Middle Ages by the more maneuverable rudder.

To sail against the wind sailing ships must make a zigzag course called tacking. The triangular lateen sail allows the ship to sail closer into the wind, getting farther ahead on the same number of tacks as the square-rigged ship.

Wind direction

Northern clinker-built hull section

Southern carvel-built hull section

A Norse longship, and a Mediterranean carrack (Columbus' *Santa Maria*)

Shipbuilding was greatly improved during the Middle Ages. Ships adopted stronger carvel hulls, as well as the Mediterranean lateen sail, which pointed better into the wind. Aboard a ship like this one brave sailors of the fourteenth and fifteenth centuries ventured out on the oceans of the world.

The first compasses may have been used in China, entering Europe via Arab traders on the Indian Ocean. A piece of naturally occurring lodestone, which is magnetic, served as the earliest compass needle. Fitted to a splinter of wood, floating on water, it would always point to the north magnetic pole. It was a major aid to navigation.

A compass rose

horseshoes. Stirrups made riding easier, and the mounted soldier now had the leverage to strike a forceful blow with his lance.

Mills powered by water or wind, and using ingenious gearing, sprang up all over the place to grind grain, pump water and saw wood.

Ships were built stronger, and were equipped with true rudders and lateen sails, which gave them the strength and maneuverability to sail the high seas. The novel compass guided the mariner on his way.

In spite of their widespread use, the origins of these inventions went undocumented. It would seem, though, that many came from the East: Asia, China and the Arab world. These lands also brought to Europe, via adventurous overland traders, silks and spices, and legends of splendid, golden cities. The prospect of wealth, free for the taking, prompted the royal houses of Europe to seek sea routes to the "treasure chests" of the East. While searching for gold, they discovered the world!

75

Conquest and Exploration

Judging from maps of the period, such as the Ptolemaic map on page 12, the world known to medieval Europeans was a small and cozy place. Yet although on paper the "world's edge" appeared to lie just beyond the horizon, Europeans were in contact with goods brought from well off the map . . . from the Indies, and the Orient.

Although no one from Europe had really been there, people knew of it from Arab traders who plied the coastal waters of the

This map shows the then known world of the early 1500s.

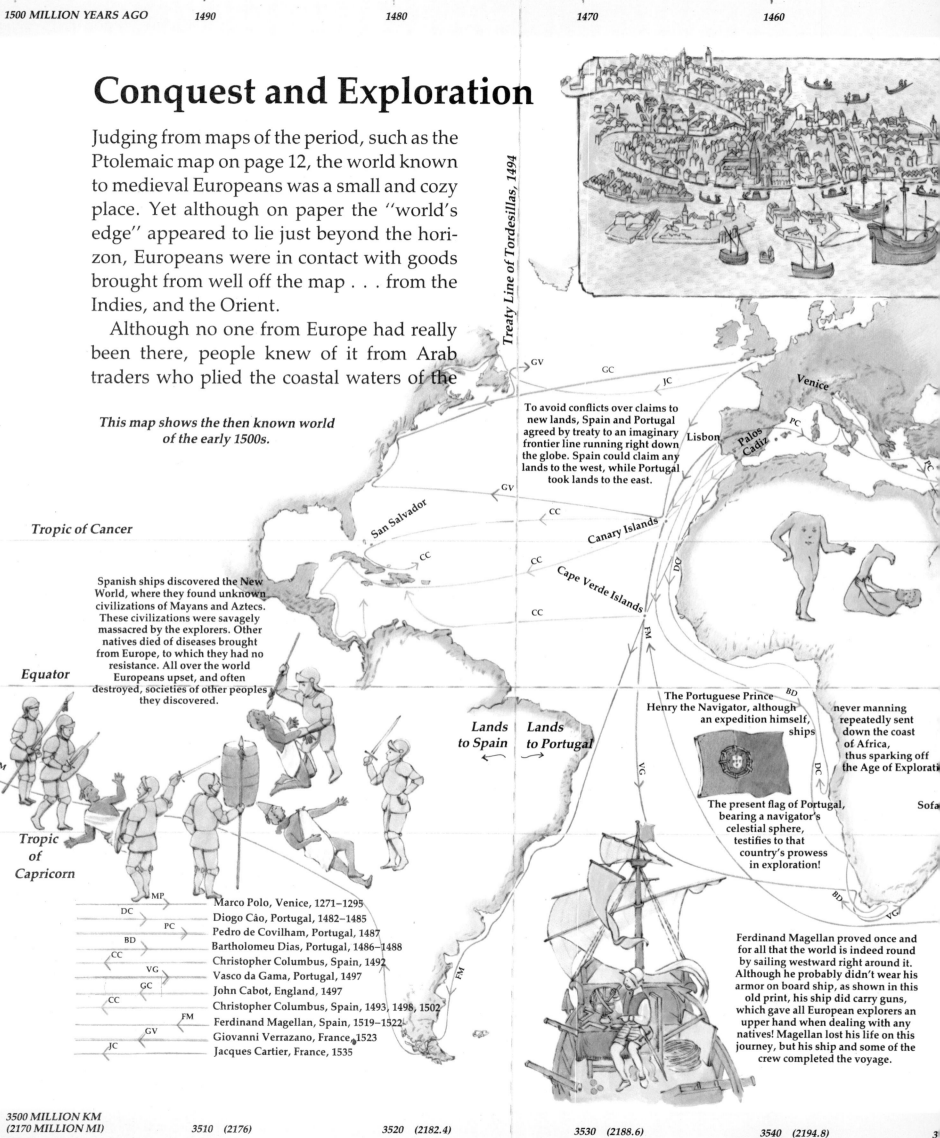

Treaty Line of Tordesillas, 1494

To avoid conflicts over claims to new lands, Spain and Portugal agreed by treaty to an imaginary frontier line running right down the globe. Spain could claim any lands to the west, while Portugal took lands to the east.

Spanish ships discovered the New World, where they found unknown civilizations of Mayans and Aztecs. These civilizations were savagely massacred by the explorers. Other natives died of diseases brought from Europe, to which they had no resistance. All over the world Europeans upset, and often destroyed, societies of other peoples they discovered.

The Portuguese Prince Henry the Navigator, although never manning an expedition himself, repeatedly sent ships down the coast of Africa, thus sparking off the Age of Exploration!

The present flag of Portugal, bearing a navigator's celestial sphere, testifies to that country's prowess in exploration!

Lands to Spain ←   Lands to Portugal →

Tropic of Cancer

Equator

Tropic of Capricorn

San Salvador

Canary Islands

Cape Verde Islands

Venice

Lisbon   Palos   Cadiz

Sofa

Marco Polo, Venice, 1271–1295
Diogo Cão, Portugal, 1482–1485
Pedro de Covilham, Portugal, 1487
Bartholomeu Dias, Portugal, 1486–1488
Christopher Columbus, Spain, 1492
Vasco da Gama, Portugal, 1497
John Cabot, England, 1497
Christopher Columbus, Spain, 1493, 1498, 1502
Ferdinand Magellan, Spain, 1519–1522
Giovanni Verrazano, France, 1523
Jacques Cartier, France, 1535

Ferdinand Magellan proved once and for all that the world is indeed round by sailing westward right around it. Although he probably didn't wear his armor on board ship, as shown in this old print, his ship did carry guns, which gave all European explorers an upper hand when dealing with any natives! Magellan lost his life on this journey, but his ship and some of the crew completed the voyage.

Indian Ocean and brought to the Eastern Mediterranean ports exotic and rare goods from the East, and doubtless no less fabulous tales.

The powerful cities of Genoa and Venice held a monopoly on trade in the Eastern Mediterranean, and it was through these cities that silks, spices, pepper, tea, gold and ivory found their way into Europe. It was from Venice that the young Marco joined his father, a trader named Nicolo Polo, on a journey by land into Asia. Their trip took them all the way to China, and Marco returned home aged only twenty-four years. He wrote of his amazing adventures in strange lands in a book called *Il Milione*, and his experiences became known all over Europe.

A copy of Marco Polo's book fell into the hands of a Portuguese prince in 1428. Already imbued with a spirit for discovery, and sending sailing expeditions southward along the coast of Africa, it occurred to him that if one sailed far enough, one might actually round the African continent and sail eastward to the riches of the Orient, breaking the Venetian monopoly on trade with the East. Later known as Henry the Navigator, the prince sent ships farther and farther away, and after his death a Portuguese ship, sailed by Vasco da Gama, finally reached the Indian shore.

The Spanish royal house, also tempted by the possibility of enrichment through eastern trade, consented to equip a Genovese navigator who claimed India could be reached by sailing west. Indeed, the sailor Columbus did touch land, but instead of finding India, he found a New World. Spain found that this new territory held riches of its own, and began setting up colonies all around it.

The oceans soon teemed with ships under many flags: Dutch, English, French, all seeking ports with which to trade, and lands to claim as colonies. There were lands of every description: in size, shape and color . . . and as many different types of people, too! 77

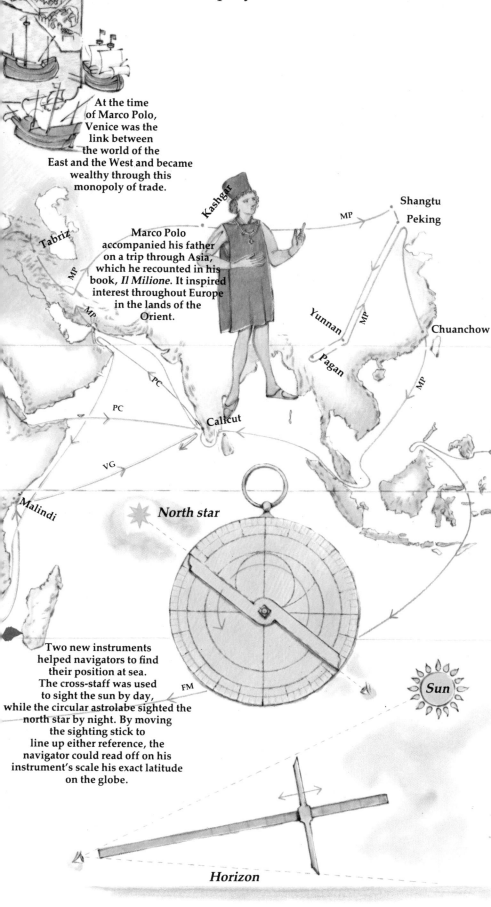

At the time of Marco Polo, Venice was the link between the world of the East and the West and became wealthy through this monopoly of trade.

Marco Polo accompanied his father on a trip through Asia, which he recounted in his book, *Il Milione*. It inspired interest throughout Europe in the lands of the Orient.

Two new instruments helped navigators to find their position at sea. The cross-staff was used to sight the sun by day, while the circular astrolabe sighted the north star by night. By moving the sighting stick to line up either reference, the navigator could read off on his instrument's scale his exact latitude on the globe.

North star

Sun

Horizon

Variety and Acceptance

The explorers who pushed back the horizons of the globe and discovered new lands also found different types of people wherever they went. In some places the native inhabitants were generally tall; in others, they were short. The shape of their eyes, the color of their skin and of their hair was different.

What makes people around the world different? Anthropologists today believe that there was no original human type, but that people developed biological characteristics best suited to their environment, depending on where they lived. Very ancient human fossils found around the world, showing different bone structures, support this theory. People with biological differences are known as different races, although all the different races belong to the one species, Homo sapiens.

When Europeans colonized the world in the sixteenth and seventeenth centuries, the original local races became mixed with the European one, giving us the endless variety of types of people we can see around the world today.

The color of people's skin or their physical characteristics are not the only ways in which they might be different from others.

There is another, invisible, distinguishing feature. In 1900 it was discovered that there are four different types or groups of blood. Each of us inherits his blood group from one of his parents. It was found that some blood types were more predominant in some places of the world than others, just as skin types are.

People of different races have tended to nurture a mutual dislike for one another. People often dislike, or fear, what they don't know, or what is unusual to them. People who are hostile to another race are called racist. They are always finding fault in other races, perhaps to cover up their own doubts about themselves!

Acceptance (and not just tolerance) of all the different peoples of the earth, and respect for their ways and customs, shows you have real understanding for the whole world . . . not just a personal view.

No one of us is superior or inferior, and if we are all a bit different, so much the better! It would be boring if everyone were the same.

Do you like ice cream? If so, you are probably delighted that there are more flavors than just vanilla!

78

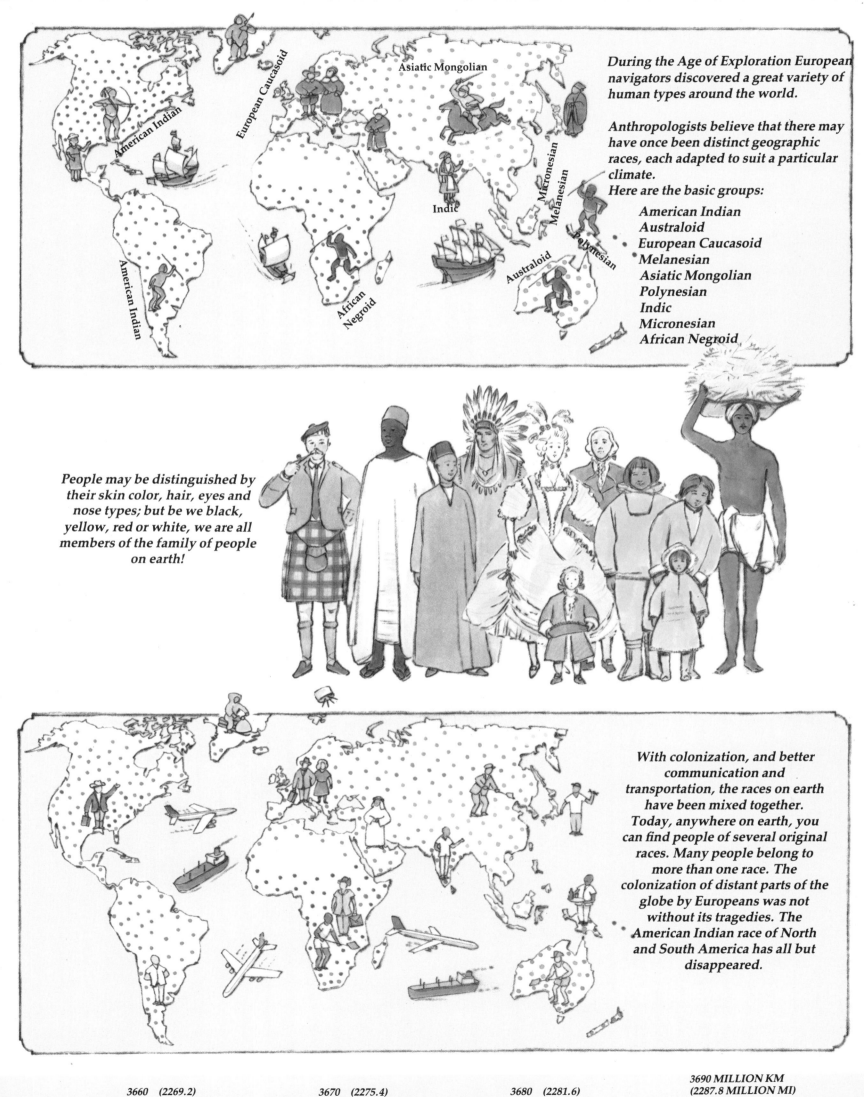

During the Age of Exploration European navigators discovered a great variety of human types around the world.

Anthropologists believe that there may have once been distinct geographic races, each adapted to suit a particular climate.

Here are the basic groups:

American Indian
Australoid
European Caucasoid
Melanesian
Asiatic Mongolian
Polynesian
Indic
Micronesian
African Negroid

People may be distinguished by their skin color, hair, eyes and nose types; but be we black, yellow, red or white, we are all members of the family of people on earth!

With colonization, and better communication and transportation, the races on earth have been mixed together. Today, anywhere on earth, you can find people of several original races. Many people belong to more than one race. The colonization of distant parts of the globe by Europeans was not without its tragedies. The American Indian race of North and South America has all but disappeared.

Function and Expression

From the moment that man made his very first tool, he has been an artist. In remaking his environment to suit his needs, he took natural objects out of their context, and reorganized them, or transformed them to his imaginative wishes. Nature, however beautiful it is, is never art. Only man makes art, and he does it by transforming nature. Of course, not everything man makes can be called art . . . far from it! So what does art mean?

Defining art is much less easy than recognizing it. Each one of us, with his individual background and sensitivity, could give a quite different definition. Even just recognizing art is largely a matter of personal taste!

Some things, like painting and sculpture, are done deliberately as works of art, to be admired for their beauty or for what they express. Other things are made with a practical function, but we can still admire the artistry of fine craftsmanship and sensitive proportions. Early man, for instance, made his arrowheads with such skill that we can find artistry in their design. The man who made them, however, may not have given art a moment's thought!

Although this is over-simplifying things, something done artistically is something done well. Artistry might be defined as something done in an outstanding way!

Of all the different arts, architecture best combines the dual beauty of function and expression. The first purpose of a building is to serve a function: to house some sort of activity within it. Churches, or houses, or factories look alike because they all do the same job. If a building is well suited to its

Birth of Venus, by Sandro Botticelli, about 1485

Reclining figure, by Henry Moore, 1945–6

The human figure, and the nude in particular, is important subject matter in Western art. Oil painting gives a realistic rendering of space, volume and surface: a goal which Western painters sought in a scientific manner. However, artists do not alw[ays] seek realistic representation, but ofte[n] synthesize what they have seen int[o] abstract forms which become purely expressive.

Islamic bowl, 10th century

Anatolian carpet, circa 1600

The Islamic religion shuns the pictorial representation of humans, so much Islamic art is non-figurative. Highly decorative tapestry is a hallmark of Islamic art, and calligraphy, the art of fine writing, such as on this bowl, is considered an important art.

purpose, it has lived up to the first beauty, that of function. If, at the same time, it has been built with care and thought, with pleasing proportions and appropriate materials, the building has become expressive.

Society prescribes the role architecture takes. Buildings can tell us much about the people who used them. The great pyramids of Ancient Egypt, the cathedrals of the

80

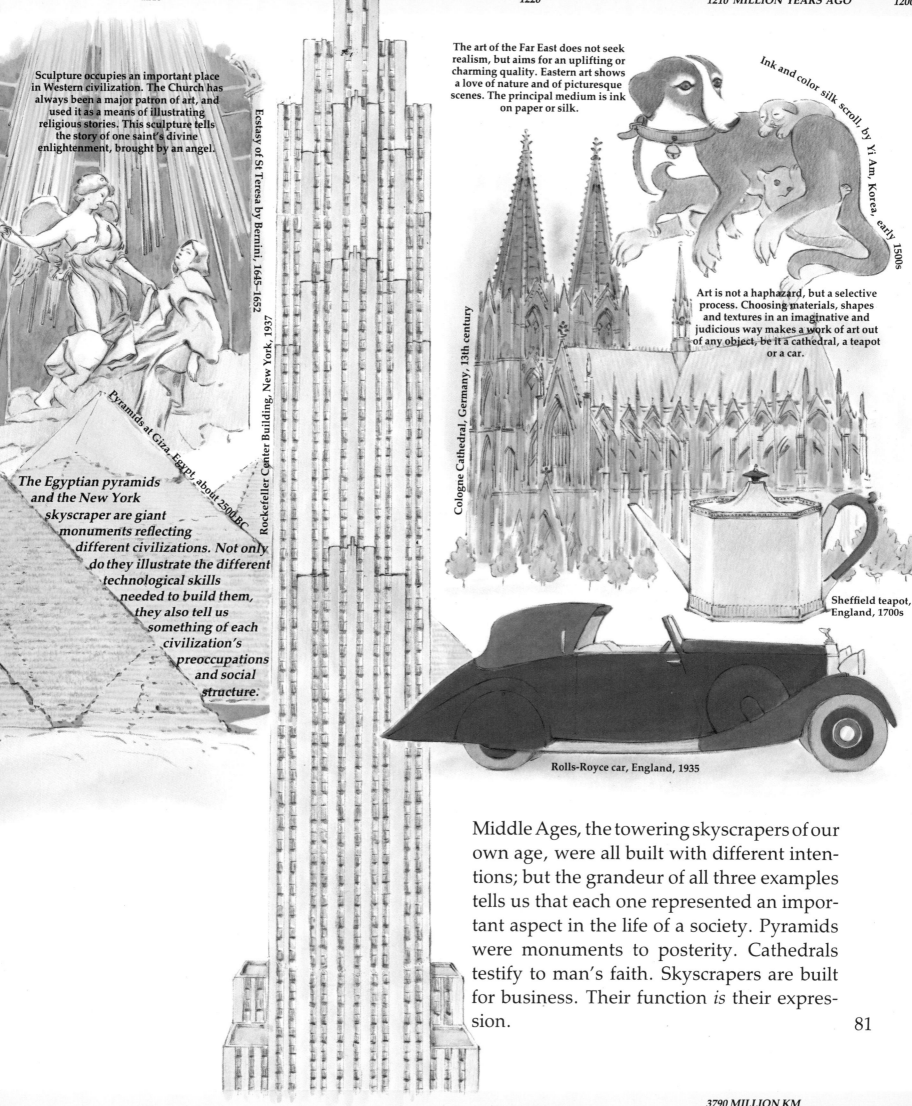

Sculpture occupies an important place in Western civilization. The Church has always been a major patron of art, and used it as a means of illustrating religious stories. This sculpture tells the story of one saint's divine enlightenment, brought by an angel.

Ecstasy of St Teresa by Bernini, 1645–1652

The art of the Far East does not seek realism, but aims for an uplifting or charming quality. Eastern art shows a love of nature and of picturesque scenes. The principal medium is ink on paper or silk.

Ink and color silk scroll, by Yi Am, Korea, early 1500s

Pyramids at Giza, Egypt, about 2500 BC

Rockefeller Center Building, New York, 1937

Art is not a haphazard, but a selective process. Choosing materials, shapes and textures in an imaginative and judicious way makes a work of art out of any object, be it a cathedral, a teapot or a car.

Cologne Cathedral, Germany, 13th century

The Egyptian pyramids and the New York skyscraper are giant monuments reflecting different civilizations. Not only do they illustrate the different technological skills needed to build them, they also tell us something of each civilization's preoccupations and social structure.

Sheffield teapot, England, 1700s

Rolls-Royce car, England, 1935

Middle Ages, the towering skyscrapers of our own age, were all built with different intentions; but the grandeur of all three examples tells us that each one represented an important aspect in the life of a society. Pyramids were monuments to posterity. Cathedrals testify to man's faith. Skyscrapers are built for business. Their function *is* their expression.

81

Rhythm and Punctuation

Painting, sculpture and architecture are known as spatial arts, for they owe their existence to a play of surfaces and volumes, light and shadow, which occupy space. Art, however, is not confined to spatial dimension alone. It is also concerned with the dimension of time.

The arts of literature, poetry, music, dance and theater might all be called temporal arts, for they all make use of the passage of time to tell us a story, or arouse our emotions.

A good storyteller will manipulate time, punctuating some passages with details or wit, to build up our interest in his tale before unveiling its outcome. A writer does just the same, but through the medium of the printed word. A poet uses time rather like a musician or dancer, giving his words a rhythm and rhyme, tickling our mind through a careful selection of words.

Music is unlike any other art, for in no way does it imitate, or refer to, any audible or visual thing in nature. Music speaks directly to our emotions. We feel some music as happy, other pieces as sad, or serious. Music sounds fast, slow, boisterous or gentle. Music is the art which is perhaps most strongly concerned with time, with its measured cadence and regularly repeated rhythm. It also serves as a support, or accompaniment, to other arts: song, dance and theater.

Dancing may well be the oldest of all the arts, originating in the natural urge to move and jump to the sound of clapping hands or drumbeats. Dances have also been used all over the world, and since ancient times, as rituals to ensure nature's assistance and

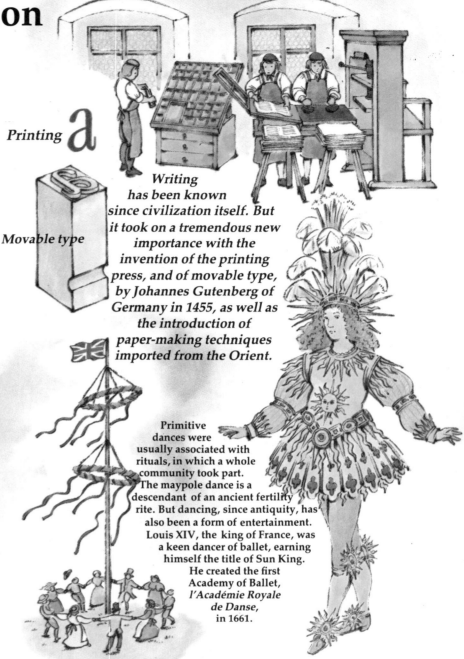

Printing

Movable type

Writing has been known since civilization itself. But it took on a tremendous new importance with the invention of the printing press, and of movable type, by Johannes Gutenberg of Germany in 1455, as well as the introduction of paper-making techniques imported from the Orient.

Primitive dances were usually associated with rituals, in which a whole community took part. The maypole dance is a descendant of an ancient fertility rite. But dancing, since antiquity, has also been a form of entertainment. Louis XIV, the king of France, was a keen dancer of ballet, earning himself the title of Sun King. He created the first Academy of Ballet, l'Académie Royale de Danse, in 1661.

goodness to man. It was probably as a derivation, or even parody, of such ritual spectacles that the theater itself was born.

Like so many beautiful things – a flower, a ripe fruit, a rainbow – the temporal arts last but an instant; and unless they can be somehow preserved, they are only as lasting as our memory. Today we take for granted our records, tapes, television, radio and movies,

82

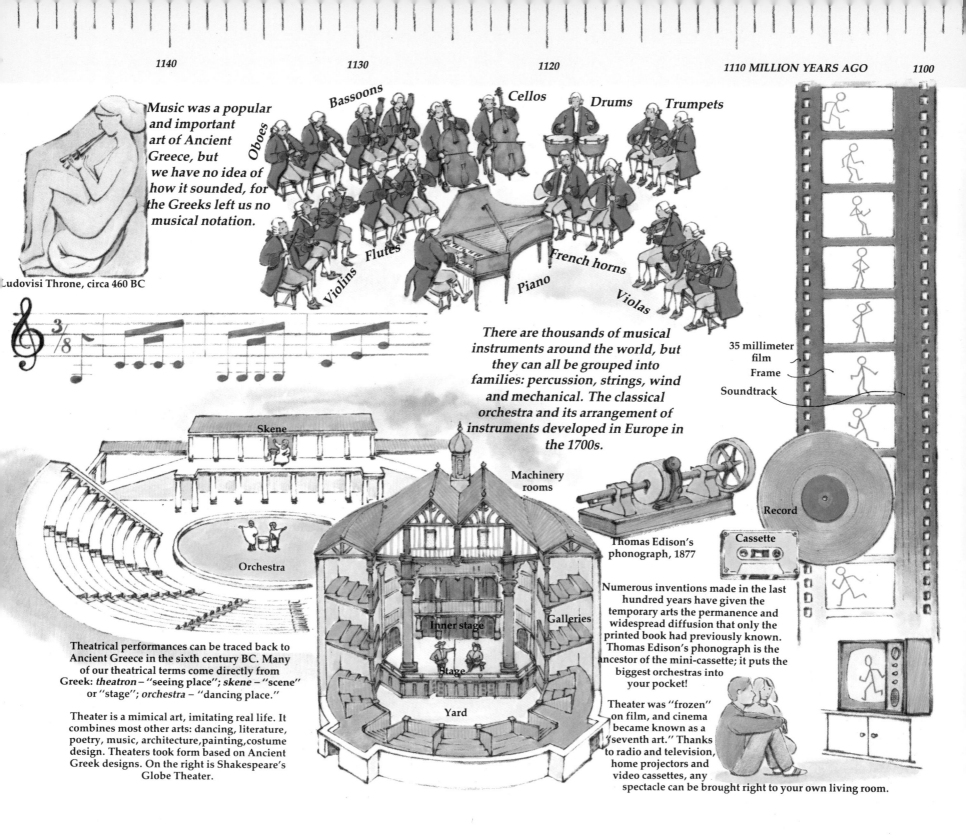

Music was a popular and important art of Ancient Greece, but we have no idea of how it sounded, for the Greeks left us no musical notation.

Ludovisi Throne, circa 460 BC

Oboes   Bassoons   Cellos   Drums   Trumpets

Violins   Flutes   Piano   French horns   Violas

There are thousands of musical instruments around the world, but they can all be grouped into families: percussion, strings, wind and mechanical. The classical orchestra and its arrangement of instruments developed in Europe in the 1700s.

35 millimeter film
Frame
Soundtrack

Skene

Machinery rooms

Orchestra

Inner stage

Stage

Galleries

Yard

Record

Thomas Edison's phonograph, 1877

Cassette

Theatrical performances can be traced back to Ancient Greece in the sixth century BC. Many of our theatrical terms come directly from Greek: *theatron* – "seeing place"; *skene* – "scene" or "stage"; *orchestra* – "dancing place."

Theater is a mimical art, imitating real life. It combines most other arts: dancing, literature, poetry, music, architecture, painting, costume design. Theaters took form based on Ancient Greek designs. On the right is Shakespeare's Globe Theater.

Numerous inventions made in the last hundred years have given the temporary arts the permanence and widespread diffusion that only the printed book had previously known. Thomas Edison's phonograph is the ancestor of the mini-cassette; it puts the biggest orchestras into your pocket!

Theater was "frozen" on film, and cinema became known as a "seventh art." Thanks to radio and television, home projectors and video cassettes, any spectacle can be brought right to your own living room.

which keep us in constant touch with the temporal arts. It is hard to imagine what it would be like to live without these inventions . . . and yet they are all only one or two generations old.

Without records the only music we would know would be what we could hear played live. We would have to go to a theater whenever we wanted to see a play. And just imagine if there were no books! Why, the only stories we'd know would be those we were told!

Recording, through printed words, tapes and films, has given us an immeasurably larger library of artistic knowledge than any of our ancestors could possibly have hoped to grasp in a lifetime. Don't you think we're lucky?

83

God and Religion

The Ancient Egyptians believed that different gods held different powers. This falcon, Horus, for instance, was the god of the king. The pharaoh himself was revered as a god, responsible for all the order in the world.

Christianity is the religion of Christ, the Messiah, who is believed by his followers to be the Son of God, who rose from the dead. Christ was crucified by Roman soldiers who at that time governed Palestine. His teachings were recorded by his apostles. Christianity is the most widespread religion in the world today.

Judaism is one of the oldest religions in the world, and believed to be the first to teach belief in one god only. The Menorah candlestick is a symbol of the Jewish faith.

Buddha, the Enlightened One, is the title given to an Ancient Indian prince who spent his life in the quest for truth. His teachings gave rise to Buddhism, a religion spread throughout eastern Asia.

The Ancient Chinese yin-yang symbol illustrates the duality found everywhere within the sphere of the universe: life-death, light-darkness, up-down, and so on.

Mollusk shell

Quartz crystal

Diatom (algae)

Order is found everywhere in nature. The beautiful construction of a mollusk's shell; the geometric design of a minute diatom; the symmetry of a snowflake – all are amazing examples of the order found throughout the natural world. Is this order the outcome of pure hazard . . .

Today we have more knowledge about the earth and the universe than any previous generation. What has knowledge taught us? You might think that it makes us feel smart, but in fact knowledge makes us very humble.

Physicists have broken down atoms into even smaller particles, and they still haven't met the ultimate ''brick'' of all matter. Astronomers are pushing back the horizon of the universe in space and time but have come nowhere nearer its ''edge.'' When men knew very little of the physical world, they explained things through theories. But now, with so much more knowledge, we can only account for how little we really know!

Throughout history, and around the world, people have always accounted for what they couldn't understand as the work or will of God. God has been given many shapes and many different names but he is generally believed to be a supreme being

84

Our knowledge of the physical universe might be likened to our perception of light waves. Our eyes can see only the narrow section of visible light, from ultraviolet to infrared. Our knowledge of the universe is limited by our technological means. At either end of the physical scale, from the infinitely small to the infinitely great, there lies much more beyond. We cannot yet attain it, but we sense its presence. This "moreness" of space and time supports man's sense of God.

Snowflake

. . . or is there more to nature than that?

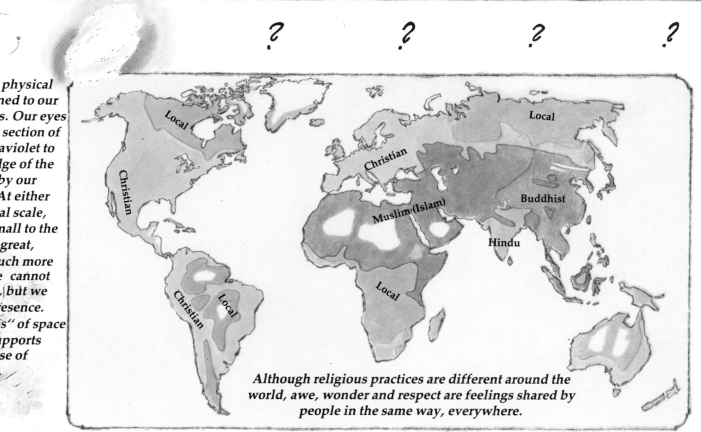

Although religious practices are different around the world, awe, wonder and respect are feelings shared by people in the same way, everywhere.

who has created all the order in the universe.

Men use language to communicate with one another. Religion is a communication between man and God. Languages are based on many different symbols which make up an alphabet, all arranged according to rules to make a common grammar. Religions make use of all sorts of symbols through which man seeks communication with God. Religious symbols are also arranged and used according to rules. These make up a common grammar for all users of a religion to follow.

Like languages, all religions are made by man. Although they are different the world over, no one religion is better than another: each speaks in its own way to God.

You have probably heard people discussing whether God exists or not. Everyone seems to have an argument defending his own point of view. The truth is, however, that no one really knows.

85

Mores and Culture

As well as being a vehicle of communication, most religions also serve as a basis of conduct in our daily lives. Religions lay down guidelines which advise us how we should live. Such guidelines, defended by society, are called mores, from the Latin word for custom.

Mores are customs which have been handed down over many generations, and to which society has attached an almost sacred importance. In the Christian world, mores permit a man to have one wife only; whereas in the Islamic world, he may have several. The Islamic man, however, is allowed no alcohol – his mores forbid it.

Lesser customs, such as tipping one's hat or shaking a hand, are known as folkways.

We have looked at the fruit of human thought: language, art, architecture, music, technology, religion. All these things, and many more, make up what is called culture. Culture is the sum of elements that make up a particular way of life for a whole society. Culture is inherited. Each one of us has to

When we play a game we abide by a mutual set of rules which make the game possible. Without rules the game cannot be played. In life each person abides by common rules, moral or legal, which allow the community to live peacefully and harmoniously.

Codes of behavior are closely tied to religion. Moses is believed to have received the Ten Commandments directly from God while on Mount Sinai in Palestine. The Babylonian ruler Hammurabi similarly received a code of laws from the sun god Shamash. He had them written down on a stone pillar decorated with a bas-relief.

"In everything, do unto others what you would have them do unto you."

This Golden Rule, found in the Bible, is found in most other religions, too. It is called the Golden Rule because it seems to excel all other rules of conduct in its simple recognition of equal respect for all men, by all men.

learn everything from childhood: first we imitate the ways of our parents, and later we pick up the customs of all the other people around us.

There are thousands of cultures all around the earth. Each is a mixture of innovative ideas, or acceptance of change, as well as inherited traditions, or unwillingness to change.

The network and rapidity of communications today has brought each one of us into contact with cultures from all over the world.

While the customs of other people may look strange to us, many of ours must seem funny to others!

Communication has influenced every culture. A custom may be dropped by society and replaced by one from abroad. Although the mixing of cultures has "killed" some traditions, their loss has given us a renewed sensitivity towards them for their historical value.

The diversity of cultures is full of interest and beauty.

Japan is an example of a country where traditions are strongly revered. Many women, for instance, still wear the traditional kimono. At the same time the country has adopted, and often surpassed, the ways of the modern Western world, of a foreign society.

The idea of beauty is different in each society, and depends largely on handed-down and accepted traditions.

Make-up, tattoos, whiskers, hairdos, wigs, deformed lips and ears may be prized or ridiculed, depending on where and when you live!

These soldiers maintain a tradition: the protection of their Queen. The ancient custom is maintained for the respect it inspires.

87

Power and Administration

What do you do for your family? Perhaps you have certain chores which you do regularly, like cleaning the car, mowing the lawn, or doing the dishes. Maybe you even babysit for your little brother or sister. You have responsibilities, and by carrying them out you cooperate with your parents to help make a harmonious family.

The family is society's oldest institution and its basic unit. In a way, it is a miniature government. It is an exercise of cooperation among separate members towards a common goal.

There are several ways of running a family. Sometimes the father is the dominant figure, holding all the power and making all the decisions. This type of family is called patriarchal. In other cases both mother and father make decisions together, and might take notice of their children's ideas, too. Such a family is egalitarian.

The family probably served as a model for the earliest governments. At the simplest level, government is a means of cooperation among a number of families. The ways of administering a government are as different as the ways of running a family.

Throughout history, and in many places today, most governments have tended to be modelled on the patriarchal family. One person or a small group of people holds all the power and makes all decisions by themselves. Monarchies, dictatorships and

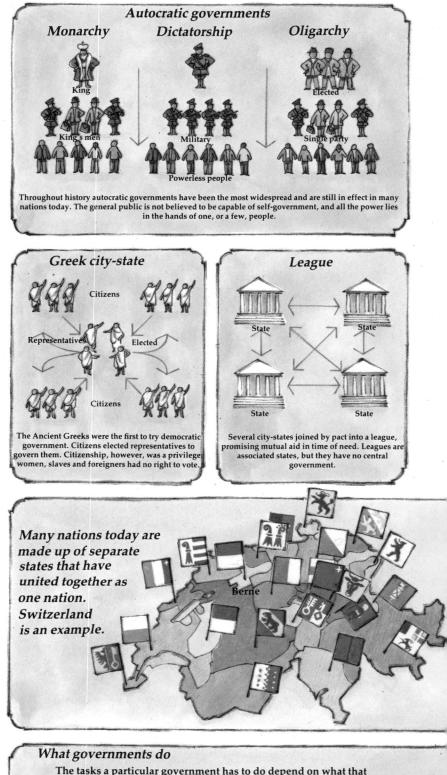

Autocratic governments

Monarchy *Dictatorship* *Oligarchy*

King   Elected

King's men Military Single party

Powerless people

Throughout history autocratic governments have been the most widespread and are still in effect in many nations today. The general public is not believed to be capable of self-government, and all the power lies in the hands of one, or a few, people.

Greek city-state

Citizens

Representatives Elected

Citizens

The Ancient Greeks were the first to try democratic government. Citizens elected representatives to govern them. Citizenship, however, was a privilege; women, slaves and foreigners had no right to vote.

League

State   State

State   State

Several city-states joined by pact into a league, promising mutual aid in time of need. Leagues are associated states, but they have no central government.

Many nations today are made up of separate states that have united together as one nation. Switzerland is an example.

Berne

What governments do

The tasks a particular government has to do depend on what that government represents. Taking Italy as an example, municipal government is concerned with looking after the well-being of a community. It is responsible for the provision of water, for sanitation, and for local transportation and schools. Roads, which serve a number of communities, fall under the administration of a provincial or regional government. Central or state government deals with matters on a national level; defense, foreign affairs, and the printing of money, for example.

Commune   Province

88

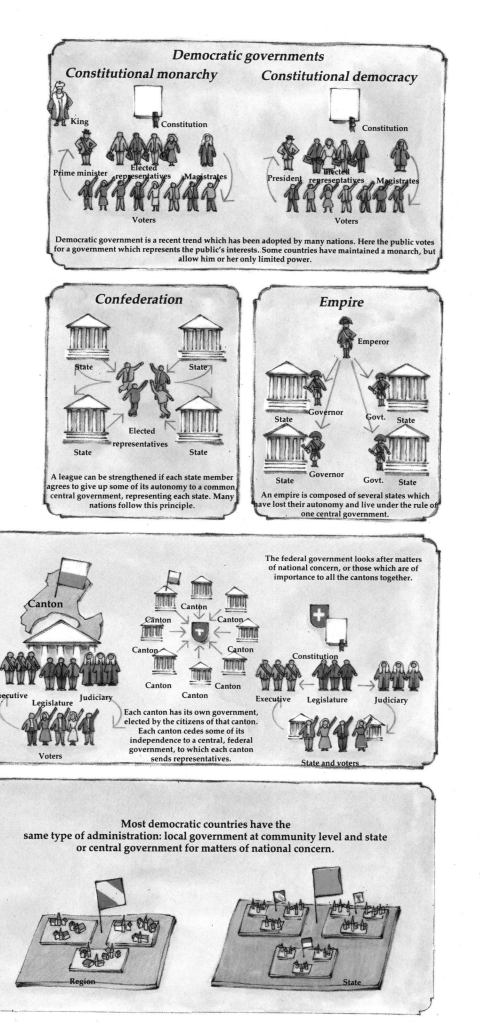

Democratic governments

Constitutional monarchy

King
Constitution
Prime minister
Elected representatives
Magistrates
Voters

Democratic government is a recent trend which has been adopted by many nations. Here the public votes for a government which represents the public's interests. Some countries have maintained a monarch, but allow him or her only limited power.

Constitutional democracy

Constitution
President
Elected representatives
Magistrates
Voters

Confederation

State
State
State
State
Elected representatives

A league can be strengthened if each state member agrees to give up some of its autonomy to a common, central government, representing each state. Many nations follow this principle.

Empire

Emperor
State
Governor
State
Govt.
State
State
Governor
State
Govt.
State

An empire is composed of several states which have lost their autonomy and live under the rule of one central government.

The federal government looks after matters of national concern, or those which are of importance to all the cantons together.

Canton
Canton
Canton
Canton
Canton
Canton
Canton
Canton
Executive   Legislature   Judiciary
Voters

Constitution
Executive   Legislature   Judiciary
State and voters

Each canton has its own government, elected by the citizens of that canton. Each canton cedes some of its independence to a central, federal government, to which each canton sends representatives.

Most democratic countries have the same type of administration: local government at community level and state or central government for matters of national concern.

Region
State

empires fall into this category.

The other type of government, more egalitarian, spreads the power by giving a share of it directly to the people governed. In history the first such governments were the Greek city-states. We call such governments democracies, from the Greek words *demos*, "people" and *kratos*, "power." A republic means the same thing, but comes from the Latin words *res publica*, or "public thing."

Most democracies were created in this century. However, in many places only the name is adopted, mock elections and single-party representation belying a government where only a few men really hold the reins.

Governments exist on every level: tribe or clan; municipal governments; cantonal or regional governments; and nations.

Nations are large groups of people who have a common bond: through geography, language, religion, an idea or common interest. Sometimes nations bond together in federations to cooperate within particular fields, such as trade or defense.

Government is not an end in itself. It acts as a service to its citizens. It provides protection, agrees to a common law and administers justice. It also carries out projects for the public good, such as building roads, schools, and hospitals. Government is a tremendous convenience to civilization . . . but it can also be a curse.

89

Fear and Aggression

We all get angry. Nearly every day there is some little thing that annoys us. If pushed too far, we feel like hitting or breaking something, or letting off a lot of noise. Usually, when our fury has calmed, we can't understand what we got all worked up about – our anger seems so silly! Have you ever wondered why we get angry at all, and why we get aggressive?

We usually get angry because something, or someone, gets in the way of our plans, or steps on our ideas. We make ourselves angry because we have our *own* idea of how things *should* be, which conflicts with the way things *are*. We are all self-centered. We all have an ego, a preconceived idea of ourselves; our ego gets stepped on, and we get angry. Anger is man-made.

People let off their anger with aggression. If you're insulted, you bark back; if you're hit, you strike back. You defend yourself. Some people are always aggressive. They bully, tease, steal or vandalize. Why? They have a hidden anger and let it out; or they have a hidden fear, some insecurity which aggressiveness covers up.

Many animals hunt for their food. They need space to hunt in. Such animals reserve territorial rights, a space to hunt that is off limits to others. If another animal infringes their right, then the defending animal will make an aggressive display to frighten off the intruder.

People, too, need food and space. We are no longer hunters, but throughout history nations have intruded on their neighbors in quest of more food, or wealth, or more land to extend their activity.

90

In this diagram one tiny cube represents one ton of explosive TNT. The average bomb used in World War II had an explosive power comparable to twenty tons of TNT, illustrated by the small block of cubes in the center. On March 9, 1945, 276 B-29 bombers dropped 2000 tons (or 2 kilotons) of TNT on the city of Tokyo, killing more than 80,000 people. On August 6 of the same year, one B-29 bomber dropped an atom (fission) bomb on the city of Hiroshima, killing some 75,000 civilians and injuring about 70,000 others. That bomb yielded 20,000 tons, or 20 kilotons, of TNT, completely burning out 4.2 square miles (11 square kilometers.)

Average "blockbuster" bomb of World War II:
20 tons

Bombs dropped on Tokyo in March, 1945:
2000 tons

The atom bomb dropped on Hiroshima in 1945:
20,000 tons (20 kilotons)

All the bombs dropped in World War II, equivalent to 2,000,000 tons, or 2 megatons. This is the power of *one* average, modern, hydrogen bomb (fusion).

We have seen in the preceding pages that it is the nature of governments to be divisive. Governments are a convenience, and it is convenient to divide their fields of action. The world is divided up into about 160 nations, each with its own government. Each nation runs its affairs its own way. Look back at

The United Nations, created in 1945, unites over 150 of the world's nations in an international parliament which among other activities seeks peaceful solutions to differences between its member nations. Although the United Nations may condemn one nation for being aggressive towards another, it has no power to enforce punishment.

US participation in World War II 1941–1945: $339,000,000,000

US defense spending in 1980 alone: $153,000,000,000

US defense spending in 1970 alone: $74,000,000,000

Hundreds of nuclear-powered submarines today ply under the world's oceans carrying the flags of several different nations as well as a heavy arsenal of nuclear missiles. These ships, able to travel for months without surfacing, are virtually undetectable . . . until they have fired a warhead.

The atom bomb is a mere toy compared to its postwar descendant, the hydrogen bomb. An H-bomb uses an atom bomb just to ignite it, creating a temperature comparable to that found on the sun! Shown in the diagram is a mediocre H-bomb of 2 megatons. This is as much as all the bombs dropped in World War II, wrapped in one little package. The Soviet Union has tested a bomb with a power of 45 megatons . . . .
It is believed that today the combined nuclear arsenal of the United States and the Soviet Union has a potential power of some 200,000 Hiroshima-type bombs. If we were to multiply the number of deaths at Hiroshima (75,000) 200,000 times, the arsenal would have potential to kill 15 billion people. But there are only 4.5 billion people on earth today. In a full nuclear exchange, everyone on earth could theoretically be killed three times over!

US participation in World War I 1917–1918: $25,000,000,000

US Civil War (both sides) 1860–1865: $5,000,000,000

What does defense cost?
Here is what some wars have cost the United States in the past compared with its annual defense budget in recent years.

pages 38 and 39, the map of the earth. Can you find any nations? Can you see any political frontiers? Nature made none. Nations are man-made; they are ideas.

Nations are like individuals: after all, they are made up of people. The people of a nation share a common bond which makes up the self-centered ego of the nation itself, sometimes called the national interest. If that national ego gets upset by an insult, a provocation, or is aggressive due to internal problems, it can get angry just like a person. It strikes out and breaks things . . . it makes war.

91

Resources and Conservation

You have seen pictures of astronauts in space. The very first missions could be counted in hours, but now men can stay aloft for several weeks. There is no food, water or air in space, so, of course, astronauts have to carry with them everything needed to live. Room for all these supplies is necessarily limited, so when they run low the mission is over, and the astronauts head home to planet earth.

Seen from space, our earth looks like a spacecraft, too. It floats alone in the deep universe carrying all the necessities of life on its back. Room on it is limited, too. The biosphere, that thin skin on the earth's surface capable of supporting life, is a tiny, delicate place, with only so much food and space to go around. The biosphere is the earth's unique wealth. No other planet, as far as we know, has one. There is air to breathe, water to drink, plants and animals; mineral riches, metals and fuels are stored within its crust. These riches provided by nature – animal, vegetable and mineral – are called natural resources.

The resources on our "spacecraft" support a very demanding and voracious "astronaut" – man himself. Since he boarded the craft, man has been rearranging it to suit himself better, and he has crowded it with offspring at a frighteningly rapid rate. He's burning all his fuel and consuming his food, water and air as if at a gargantuan banquet! His mission in space won't last long . . . reserves aboard ship are limited!

Man is a burden on the earth because he is a waster. He takes from nature, but is often incapable of returning properly what he has

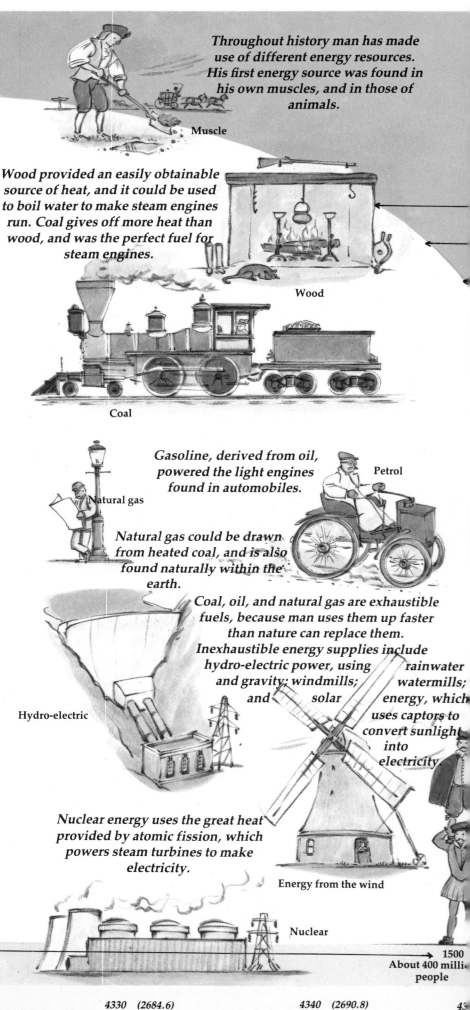

Throughout history man has made use of different energy resources. His first energy source was found in his own muscles, and in those of animals.

Muscle

Wood provided an easily obtainable source of heat, and it could be used to boil water to make steam engines run. Coal gives off more heat than wood, and was the perfect fuel for steam engines.

Wood

Coal

Natural gas

Gasoline, derived from oil, powered the light engines found in automobiles.

Petrol

Natural gas could be drawn from heated coal, and is also found naturally within the earth.

Coal, oil, and natural gas are exhaustible fuels, because man uses them up faster than nature can replace them. Inexhaustible energy supplies include hydro-electric power, using rainwater and gravity; windmills; watermills; and solar energy, which uses captors to convert sunlight into electricity.

Hydro-electric

Nuclear energy uses the great heat provided by atomic fission, which powers steam turbines to make electricity.

Energy from the wind

Nuclear

borrowed. Nature is a rejuvenating system, but it takes time. It takes thousands of years to make a seam of coal or oil; hundreds of years to make an inch of fertile soil; dozens of years to make a tall tree. But nature cannot rejuvenate if man takes away, or ruins, her building blocks.

Our spacecraft has been equipped for life, but *we* are the astronauts; each of us is responsible for our ship. If our supplies run out, there is no place to go to fetch more.

Year
2100   12 billion people

2000   6 billion and 200 million
1980   4 billion and 415 million
1950   2 billion and 513 million

1900   1 billion and 650 million

1850   1 billion and 262 million

1800   978 million

1750   791 million

1700

1650   500 million

1600

1550

Year
1500   400 million

1450

1400

1350

1300

1250

1200

1150

1100

1050

Year
1000

300 million people

950

900

Built-up, or wasteland: 14%

Arable: 3.5%

Pasture: 7%

Forests: 10.5%

Oceans: 65%

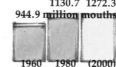

4927.1 million mouths

3284.3

2081.6 million mouths

Food production

1960   1980   (2000)
Developing countries

Increases in food production have been similar for both developed and developing countries. However the food production of the developing nations cannot keep pace with their population increase.

1130.7   1272.3
944.9 million mouths

1960   1980   (2000)
Developed countries

The earth is now supporting more than twice as many people than at the turn of the century. There may be twice as many more within the next one hundred years. 35% of the present world population is under the age of 15, while only 5.8% is over the age of 64. Millions more children will appear soon. Where will we house them; and will they find a job?

The earth's surface can be divided up roughly in the proportions shown above left. Compared with other land, very little is available for farming. Through irrigation and improved farming techniques food production can be increased, but there is nonetheless a limit to what the earth's surface can grow.

United States population: 6% of the world

United States energy consumption: 33% of the world

Remaining world population: 94%

Remaining world energy consumption: 67%

The industrialized nations of the world are the greatest users, per capita, of energy. Based on the statistics above, 6 Americans use up as much energy as 47 people elsewhere in the world.

The population explosion is illustrated by the graph above left. The great majority of births are in the developing countries of Asia.

250 years to double

1750
About 800 million people

150 years to double

1900
1 billion and 600 million people

65 years to double

1965
3 billion and 200 million people

?

6 billion and 400 million

From Cotton to Computers

Where do you live, and what do you do? Chances are that if you don't live *in* a city, you probably live near one. Your parents may work in a factory or an office, but few of us work on a farm.

Most of us live in standardized houses, with prefabricated windows and doors. Much of our food is processed and packaged in factories, and so are our clothes. Most of our information about the world around us comes from the mass media: television, radio, newspapers and magazines. We can chat with friends over the phone, hundreds of miles away!

This is a very recent way of life. Until only 200 years ago the vast majority of people lived in the country and worked on a farm. Just about everything they might need would be made in their own village: from the timber posts to make a house to the wool from which the women made clothes. People would exchange news in the village square, or at the occasional country fair, and none of their friends were much farther away than shouting distance!

What happened in between? Back on page 62, we saw how man, given certain favorable conditions, discovered how to farm. Farming totally changed man's way of life, and with it he made an agricultural civiliza-

Eli Whitney's cotton gin of 1793 separated seeds from raw cotton much faster than by hand, thus accelerating cotton production.

The Industrial Revolution began in the textile industry in the late 1700s, when Great Britain was importing raw cotton from abroad, notably from India and the new American colonies. Cotton has to be cleaned, spun and woven to make cloth. The invention of machines which took over tasks formerly done by hand sped up the production of cotton and made it cheaper. Factories were built near fast rivers so that waterwheels could provide power for the new machines.
Industry was given a real boost with the invention of the steam engine, conceived by Thomas Newcomen and fully developed and marketed by James Watt. The steam engine provided power for almost any task. Steam locomotives and steamboats improved transportation and trade developed. Coal and iron ore were mined in greater quantities to supply fuel and metal to the new, industrialized society.

tion: a diversity of jobs and trade, all thanks to the bounty of agriculture. It was an Agricultural Revolution!

Two centuries ago, starting in Britain, general conditions favored incredible new changes which revolutionized man's life just as agriculture had done centuries before. These changes are known as the Industrial Revolution: a way of life devoted to industry, and made possible by it. The great discovery of the Industrial Revolution was

94

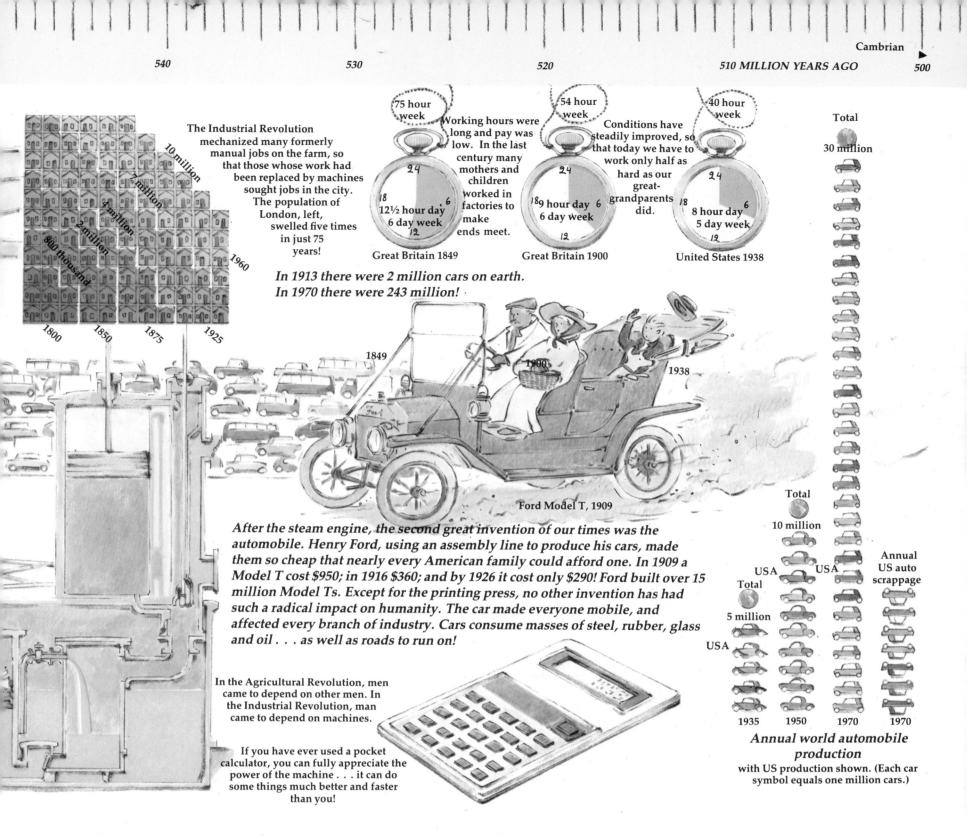

The Industrial Revolution mechanized many formerly manual jobs on the farm, so that those whose work had been replaced by machines sought jobs in the city. The population of London, left, swelled five times in just 75 years!

10 million · 6 million · 4 million · 2 million · 800 thousand
1800 · 1850 · 1875 · 1925 · 1960

75 hour week — Working hours were long and pay was low. In the last century many mothers and children worked in factories to make ends meet.
24 · 18 · 6 · 12½ hour day 6 day week · 12
Great Britain 1849

54 hour week — Conditions have steadily improved, so that today we have to work only half as hard as our great-grandparents did.
24 · 18 · 9 hour day · 6 day week · 6 · 12
Great Britain 1900

40 hour week
24 · 18 · 8 hour day 5 day week · 6 · 12
United States 1938

Total — 30 million

In 1913 there were 2 million cars on earth.
In 1970 there were 243 million!

1849 · 1900 · 1938

Ford Model T, 1909

After the steam engine, the second great invention of our times was the automobile. Henry Ford, using an assembly line to produce his cars, made them so cheap that nearly every American family could afford one. In 1909 a Model T cost $950; in 1916 $360; and by 1926 it cost only $290! Ford built over 15 million Model Ts. Except for the printing press, no other invention has had such a radical impact on humanity. The car made everyone mobile, and affected every branch of industry. Cars consume masses of steel, rubber, glass and oil . . . as well as roads to run on!

In the Agricultural Revolution, men came to depend on other men. In the Industrial Revolution, man came to depend on machines.

If you have ever used a pocket calculator, you can fully appreciate the power of the machine . . . it can do some things much better and faster than you!

Total — 10 million
Total — 5 million
USA · USA · USA · USA
Annual US auto scrappage
1935 · 1950 · 1970 · 1970

Annual world automobile production
with US production shown. (Each car symbol equals one million cars.)

that machines could do work quicker, better and cheaper. Everything in people's lives, at some point, was handled by machines. Clothes were made by machines; wheat was harvested by machines; merchandise, and people themselves, were transported by mechanical machines. Man had made an industrial civilization.

We live in it still today. The superiority of a machine's work to a man's has meant that each time a new machine was invented, the man lost his job. This is still happening today.

Machines today not only do mechanical work faster, they can "think" faster too, retrieving information and performing complicated calculations in the blink of an eye. In the past, because machines increased production, lowered prices, and thus increased demand, people put out of work were eventually reintegrated into another job. Will this be the case in the future?

95

759) 4460 (2765.2) 4470 (2771.4) 4480 (2777.6) **4490 MILLION KM (2783.8 MILLION MI)** 4500

Neptune: (2788 million miles [4497 million km] from the sun.)

Inquiry and Investigation

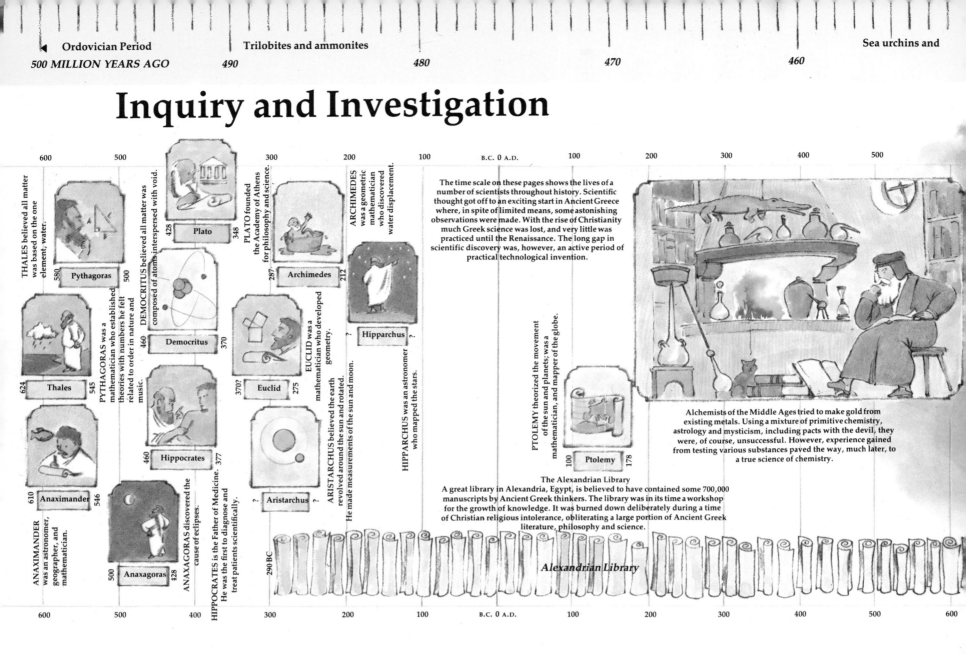

The time scale on these pages shows the lives of a number of scientists throughout history. Scientific thought got off to an exciting start in Ancient Greece where, in spite of limited means, some astonishing observations were made. With the rise of Christianity much Greek science was lost, and very little was practiced until the Renaissance. The long gap in scientific discovery was, however, an active period of practical technological invention.

THALES believed all matter was based on the one element, water.

PYTHAGORAS was a mathematician who established theories with numbers he felt related to order in nature and music.

DEMOCRITUS believed all matter was composed of atoms interspersed with void.

PLATO founded the Academy of Athens for philosophy and science.

ARCHIMEDES was a geometric mathematician who discovered water displacement.

EUCLID was a mathematician who developed geometry.

ARISTARCHUS believed the earth revolved around the sun and rotated. He made measurements of the sun and moon.

HIPPARCHUS was an astronomer who mapped the stars.

PTOLEMY theorized the movement of the sun and planets; was a mathematician, and mapper of the globe.

ANAXIMANDER was an astronomer, geographer, and mathematician.

HIPPOCRATES is the Father of Medicine. He was the first to diagnose and treat patients scientifically.

ANAXAGORAS discovered the cause of eclipses.

Alchemists of the Middle Ages tried to make gold from existing metals. Using a mixture of primitive chemistry, astrology and mysticism, including pacts with the devil, they were, of course, unsuccessful. However, experience gained from testing various substances paved the way, much later, to a true science of chemistry.

The Alexandrian Library
A great library in Alexandria, Egypt, is believed to have contained some 700,000 manuscripts by Ancient Greek thinkers. The library was in its time a workshop for the growth of knowledge. It was burned down deliberately during a time of Christian religious intolerance, obliterating a large portion of Ancient Greek literature, philosophy and science.

Alexandrian Library

Everyone loves a detective story. We marvel how, presented with some mystery, the detective searches for clues, cross-examines his bits of information to test their validity, and then unravels the whole story to us . . . the mystery brilliantly solved!

The story of our earth is a great and complex one. It is over four and a half billion years old, and the universe far older still. But Homo sapiens arrived only some fifty thousand years ago. Why, he's missed the whole show!

It was never easy for man to understand the earth on which he lived. Some things worked regularly, like the seasons, and others were totally unpredictable, like a rainstorm or an earthquake, so that understanding the earth was impossibly complex. Throughout history man has sought to explain the seemingly dual order and disorder of nature as the work and whimsy of gods. The rising sun was the work of God, and so was a flood. Man lived by mysticism and superstition, but came no closer to finding concrete answers to the mysteries around him.

A few people, however, are born detectives. They need concrete answers, and use concrete means to find them. We call such detectives scientists. Fortunately, nature has

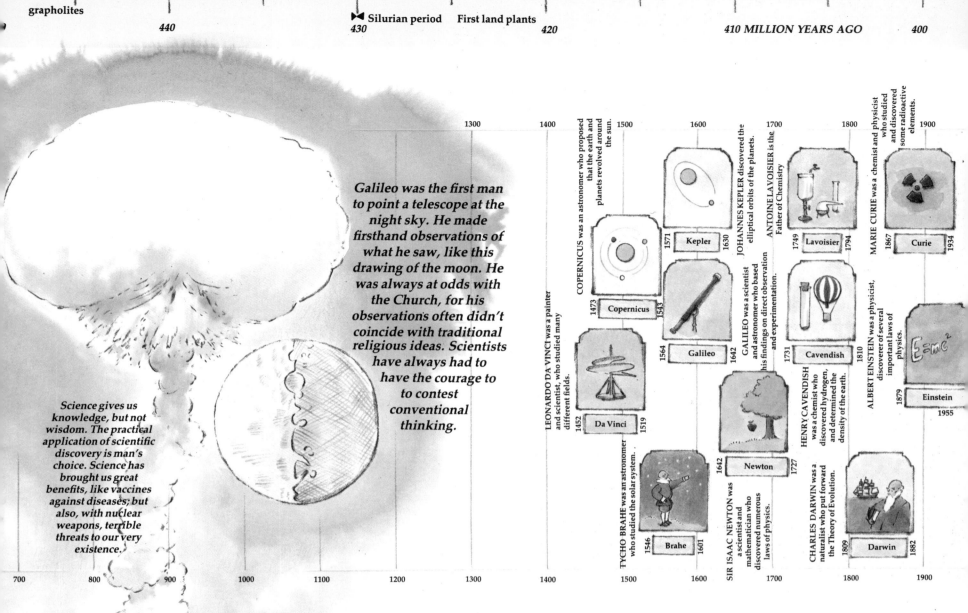

1300   1400   1500   1600   1700   1800   1900

Galileo was the first man to point a telescope at the night sky. He made firsthand observations of what he saw, like this drawing of the moon. He was always at odds with the Church, for his observations often didn't coincide with traditional religious ideas. Scientists have always had to have the courage to to contest conventional thinking.

Science gives us knowledge, but not wisdom. The practical application of scientific discovery is man's choice. Science has brought us great benefits, like vaccines against diseases; but also, with nuclear weapons, terrible threats to our very existence.

COPERNICUS was an astronomer who proposed that the earth and planets revolved around the sun.

1571 | Kepler | 1630
JOHANNES KEPLER discovered the elliptical orbits of the planets.

ANTOINE LAVOISIER is the Father of Chemistry
1749 | Lavoisier | 1794

MARIE CURIE was a chemist and physicist who studied and discovered some radioactive elements.
1867 | Curie | 1934

LEONARDO DA VINCI was a painter and scientist, who studied many different fields.
1473 | Copernicus | 1543

1564 | Galileo | 1642
GALILEO was a scientist and astronomer who based his findings on direct observation and experimentation.

1731 | Cavendish | 1810
HENRY CAVENDISH was a chemist who discovered hydrogen, and determined the density of the earth.

ALBERT EINSTEIN was a physicist, discoverer of several important laws of physics.
$E = mc^2$
1879 | Einstein | 1955

1452 | Da Vinci | 1519

TYCHO BRAHE was an astronomer who studied the solar system.
1546 | Brahe | 1601

1642 | Newton | 1727
SIR ISAAC NEWTON was a scientist and mathematician who discovered numerous laws of physics.

CHARLES DARWIN was a naturalist who put forward the Theory of Evolution.
1809 | Darwin | 1882

700   800   900   1000   1100   1200   1300   1400   1500   1600   1700   1800   1900

given these scientists clues to work with.

Nature works by certain rules, and the earth has left some traces of its past. There are "fingerprints" in fossils, and "footprints" in the crust's folds and faults. Finding out how and why nature works is the role of science. Science provides knowledge, and it replaces ideas with facts. To practice science, all preconceived ideas have to be put aside, and the scientist has to have the courage to accept the real facts his inquiry has revealed. In the face of superstition, authoritarian religions and public opinion, little science has been practiced throughout history. It takes courage to be a scientist!

Although few of us practice science as a profession, all of us can be scientists in our everyday lives. Each of us lives by concepts: what should be and should not be. We all have opinions, ideas about this and that. But can we live like scientists, and accept the facts? We all disagree on our ideas. We all have our own point of view. But on facts there is no room for disagreement: that is the way things really are.

The universe is a very great place. This is a fact. How small our own ideas, our little concepts look, compared to its vastness! Living with facts gives you a viewpoint as wide as the universe itself.

97

Conclusion

If you're looking for a conclusion, something to round off this book, you won't find it here!

In doing this book I have tried to touch on as many subjects as I could related to our earth – its place in the universe and its past – and about ourselves, its most recent and prolific inhabitants. Of course, the book didn't have the space, and I haven't the energy, to cover every subject. Having drawn my way all through these pages, I should be happy to have arrived at its completion, and write triumphantly "The End." No, arriving here at page 98, we're really only at "The Beginning"! For this is certainly not the best book you'll find about our planet. Indeed, most of the information written here has its source in other books. At your library you'll find shelves of books which deal with the same subject, or go into one field in much more depth. This book strives to be no more than an introduction to the earth, and a personal view about where we live.

If you have looked through all the pages, perhaps you have come upon something you didn't know before, or maybe you have some question. It might be that you don't agree with something I've written. If that's the case, I couldn't be happier! Now it's up to *you* to find out. If I have encouraged you to inquire about just one thing, then all my work has been worthwhile.

Our ancestors lived largely in ignorance of the world around them. In spite of that fact, man felt he held most of the answers. Today, with so much more information at hand,

we're not quite so sure any more. In the past, our ancestors were quick to point out our various differences. Today, as communication mixes people from all over the world together, we are becoming aware of our similarities. As photographs of our planet come back to us from outer space, we are becoming aware of our uniqueness. As technology is robbing us of our jobs, and has the power to completely destroy us, we are becoming aware of our preciousness, and our frailty.

At some time or another we have all wished we lived at another time in history. In contrast with so many harsh realities of today, much of the past looks gentle and rosy. Sometimes we forget that for our ancestors, our past was their present, or their future. Doubtless, they found *their* times harsh, and had their own fears about the future.

For my part, I feel that *we* are the luckiest generation. No generation before us has had so much access to so much information, so many facts, so many ideas. No one has ever had such opportunity to learn, or to travel . . . and in some of the world's more open-minded regions, to voice one's views.

Looking and learning is a faculty of prime importance to man. Unlike other animals, he is born without instincts: everything has to be taught! That necessary faculty is also one of his most precious gifts, for there is no limit to what he can take in. His faculty allows him to reflect, and makes him open to change.

Of course, no one should expect a person to know everything; that has no point. But

▶◀ **Carboniferous period**
340

330

320

310 MILLION YEARS AGO

300

one thing you learn while you're learning, is that the more knowledge you eat up, the more there is to eat!

When I was a little boy, whenever my parents told me something, I would say, "I know, I know!" Today, I see that I really don't know all *that* much after all. Learning is belittling, but that's not so bad – for it leaves still more room for you to expand!

You pick up from here. Good luck to you!

99

883)

4660 (2889.2)

4670 (2895.4)

4680 (2901.6)

4690 MILLION KM
(2907.8 MILLION MI)

4700

Index

Triassic period ▶◀ Junassic period

200 MILLION YEARS AGO
Pangea begins to separate   *190*   *180*   **Dispersal of the continents**   *170*   *160*
into different continents   **creates the Atlantic Ocean**

Bibliography

If you want to find out more about something you have read in this book, here are some others which might help you.

Britannica Junior, *edited by staff of Encyclopedia Britannica, Chicago, 1980.*

The World Book Encyclopedia, *World Book-Childcraft International, Chicago, 1980.*

The Illustrated Encyclopedia of Astronomy and Space, *edited by Ian Ridpath, T. Y. Crowell, New York, 1976.*

The Discoverers – An Encyclopedia of Explorers and Exploration, *edited by Helen Delper, McGraw-Hill, New York, 1980.*

The Times Atlas of the World, *Times Books, New York, 1980.*

The Times Atlas of World History, *Hammond Inc., Maplewood, N.J.,1979.*

Cosmos, *by Carl Sagan, Random House, New York, 1980.*

Life on Earth, *by David Attenborough, Little Brown, Boston, 1981.*

The Awakening of Intelligence, *by J. Krishnamurti, Avon Books, New York, 1976.*

Formation of Rocky Mountains (USA)   Extinction of dinosaurs   Primates

The Last Million Years

We have finally reached the end of our time scale.

The pages of this book have covered a period of 5,000 million years. The scale is marked in notches, each of which represents one million years. The five thousandth notch represents the last million years.

It is no more than one shred of the ribbon that has unwound in the course of the earth's history but it is quite different from all the others . . . look how many things it conceals.

The last notch in the time scale running right through this book represents the last million years of time on earth. That notch, shown here, may not look like much, but a great many things are contained in it. If we cut along the base and magnified it many times, we would have a more detailed time ribbon, shown to the left. There is not much activity most of the way along it, until about 50,000 years ago, when suddenly there is quite a lot of activity on our planet: men at work! When we get just within 1000 years from today, the planet is so bristling with activity, that we have to magnify our ribbon still further, seen below. Our century, the very last minute shred on the scale, can be seen only through the magnifying glass. Look how much has happened in such a short time! We live a unique and exciting moment in the life of our earth!

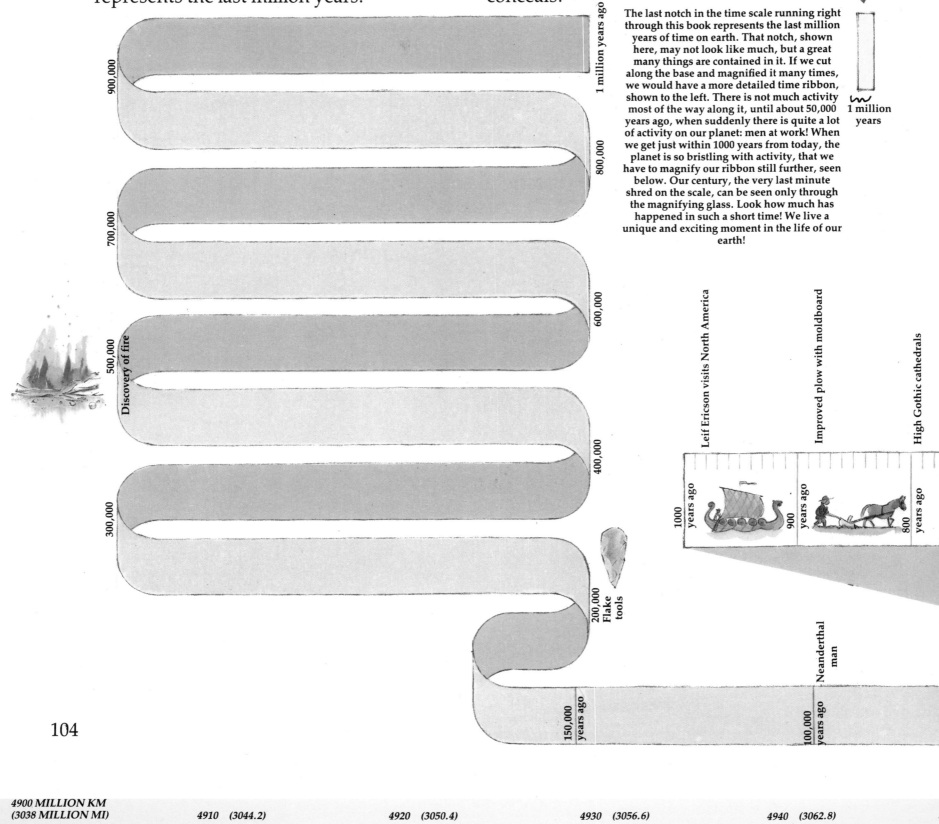

104

40 Oligocene epoch 30 Miocene epoch *20 MILLION YEARS AGO* 10 0

Formation of Himalayas

Formation of Alps

First upright ape man (3 million years ago)
First hand tools (2.5 million years ago)
Holocene epoch
Today!

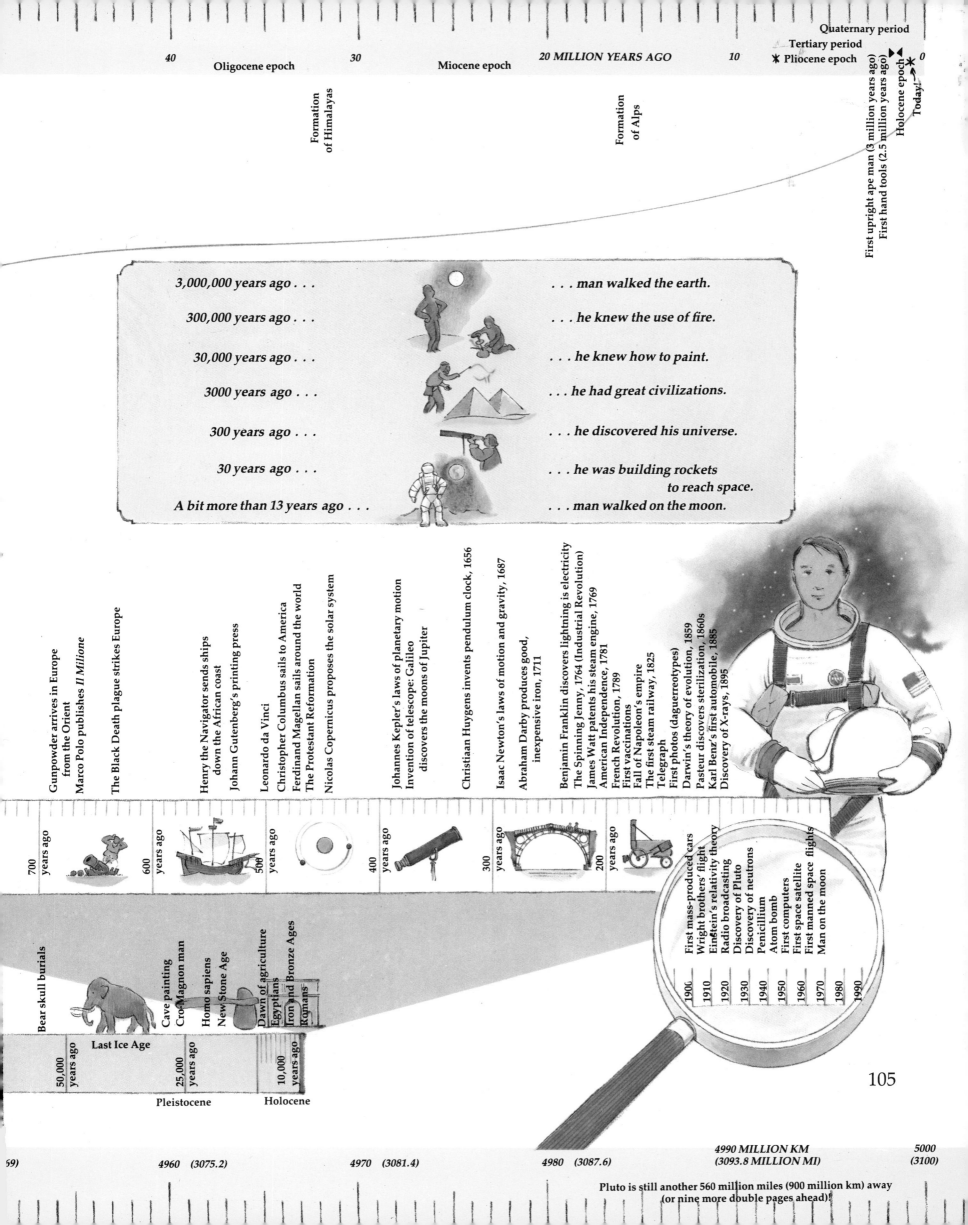

3,000,000 years ago . . .   . . . man walked the earth.

300,000 years ago . . .   . . . he knew the use of fire.

30,000 years ago . . .   . . . he knew how to paint.

3000 years ago . . .   . . . he had great civilizations.

300 years ago . . .   . . . he discovered his universe.

30 years ago . . .   . . . he was building rockets to reach space.

A bit more than 13 years ago . . .   . . . man walked on the moon.

Gunpowder arrives in Europe from the Orient
Marco Polo publishes *Il Milione*

The Black Death plague strikes Europe

Henry the Navigator sends ships down the African coast
Johann Gutenberg's printing press

Leonardo da Vinci
Christopher Columbus sails to America
Ferdinand Magellan sails around the world
The Protestant Reformation
Nicolas Copernicus proposes the solar system

Johannes Kepler's laws of planetary motion
Invention of telescope: Galileo discovers the moons of Jupiter

Christiaan Huygens invents pendulum clock, 1656

Isaac Newton's laws of motion and gravity, 1687

Abraham Darby produces good, inexpensive iron, 1711

Benjamin Franklin discovers lightning is electricity
The Spinning Jenny, 1764 (Industrial Revolution)
James Watt patents his steam engine, 1769
American Independence, 1781
French Revolution, 1789
First vaccinations
Fall of Napoleon's empire
The first steam railway, 1825
Telegraph
First photos (daguerreotypes)
Darwin's theory of evolution, 1859
Pasteur discovers sterilization, 1860s
Karl Benz's first automobile, 1885
Discovery of X-rays, 1895

700 years ago

600 years ago

500 years ago

400 years ago

300 years ago

200 years ago

First mass-produced cars
Wright brothers' flight
Einstein's relativity theory
Radio broadcasting
Discovery of Pluto
Discovery of neutrons
Penicillium
Atom bomb
First computers
First space satellite
First manned space flights
Man on the moon

1900
1910
1920
1930
1940
1950
1960
1970
1980
1990

Bear skull burials

Cave painting
Cro-Magnon man

Homo sapiens
New Stone Age

Dawn of agriculture
Egyptians
Iron and Bronze Ages
Romans

Last Ice Age

50,000 years ago

25,000 years ago

10,000 years ago

Pleistocene   Holocene

105

Pluto is still another 560 million miles (900 million km) away
(or nine more double pages ahead)!

The earth

Diameter: 7926mi (12,756km)

Distance to sun: 93,000,000mi (150,000,000km)

The moon

Diameter: 2160mi (3476km)

Distance from earth: 238,900mi (384,000km)

The earth and moon have been drawn to a scale showing their correct size and distance from the sun, which can be seen, at the same scale, on pages 2–3. The average distance between the earth and the sun is shown correctly to scale by the entire length of this book – 87 feet (26.52 meters)!

Aunt Lori
Uncle Rick

Matthew
+ Kerry

The sun

Diameter: 865,400mi (1,392,000km) Distance from earth: 92,960,000mi (149,596,000km)

The sun has been drawn here to the same scale as the earth on the last page. The average distance between the two, some 93,000,000 miles (150,000,000km), is shown, also to scale, by the entire length of the pages of this book, edge to edge: 87 (26.52m) feet long!